GARDEN LANDSCAPES IN SILK RIBBON EMBROIDERY

Garden Landscapes in Silk Ribbon Embroidery

Helen Dafter

SALLY MILNER PUBLISHING

First published in 1996 by
Sally Milner Publishing Pty Ltd
RMB 54 Burra Road
Burra Creek NSW 2620
Australia

Design and page layout by Anna Warren
Photography by Ben Wrigley
Styling by Sarah Houseman
Printed and bound in Australia by Impact Printing, Melbourne

National Library of Australia
Cataloguing in Publication Data

Dafter, Helen
Garden landscapes in silk ribbon embroidery
Includes index

ISBN 1 86351 195 4

1. Flowers in art. 2. Ribbon work. 3. Embroidery - Patterns. 4. Silk ribbon embroidery. 5. Decoration and ornament - Plant forms. I. Title. (Series : Milner craft series)

746.44041

Do not follow where the path leads,
Rather go where there is no path
and
leave
a
trail

Contents

Acknowledgements

This book, my first, has been a real challenge for me, first because of the discipline required to sit down and detail embroideries that I find so easy to create and, second, to juggle my other responsibilities to allow me free time to work on the manuscript and drawings required.

My family has helped enormously by taking up some of the tasks that have been traditionally mine as well as giving me encouragement along the way. My love and thanks to my husband Glenn and my three children Naomi, Matthew and Brian.

Silk ribbon embroidery is a relatively new craft for me although my association with traditional embroidery using stranded cotton can be traced back to a doting maternal grandmother who taught me from a very early age all the skills at which she maintained a young lady should be proficient. I no longer crochet, knit or tatt but the sewing and embroidery skills gained at such an early age have been put to good use and in many cases broadened and extended. I have a strong suspicion that my grandmother would approve of the new found skills.

Many talented students and friends over the last few years have contributed in a unique way to the contents of this book as well. Bouncing ideas backwards and forwards has forced me to explore silk ribbon embroidery even further and find a new direction for it. It certainly helps if you are surrounded by creative people who share your enthusiasm and offer constructive criticism and advice. I needn't mention them by name, they know who they are. Once again thank you for your endless support and encouragement but most of all for your friendship. It's what matters most.

It is a sincere wish of mine that this book will find a

home in some of the more remote areas of our country or indeed overseas and that people normally isolated from classes or social sewing groups will find a little inspiration from within. I find embroidery very relaxing and an ideal way of channelling creative urges. It is also a treasured pastime. If it is raining and I am unable to go out into my garden, I can turn to my current embroidery project and garden inside with never a weed in sight. This is my opportunity to give to people with like interests a little inspiration to test their own creative ability.

My thanks also to Sally Milner and staff who have made my introduction to the publication process as painless as possible.

Once again my thanks to my husband and my three children who have given me the space and opportunity to be creative. Their contributions have been endless.

This book is because of you and for you.

Helen Dafter 1996

Requirements

Before you begin any of the projects in this book read through this list of requirements carefully. Embroidery is a relaxing and fulfilling activity and having the right equipment and materials can make this pastime far less frustrating for you and increase the level of achievement you experience.

Fabric

A variety of fabrics have been chosen for the items in this book. A good quality cotton fabric, commonly known as seeded homespun forms the background for the garden landscapes. I have found this works well with the painting techniques required. Patchwork cottons and silk have been used for the other projects. The choice of fabrics is yours, however, you should make certain that you are able to pull your needle through the fabric with the required ribbon threaded — remember if you are using a 7mm silk ribbon it will be more difficult to pull through than a 2mm silk ribbon. If you are in doubt, test the fabric first.

A further point to keep in mind is the length of time you will devote to your project. It will take an equal amount of time to embroider on whatever fabric you choose, so buy the best you can afford.

Needles

I use a variety of needle sizes with my work. Generally the chenille needle is the most suitable and the larger of these, a No. 18, is used with the 7mm ribbon. You will find that the smaller sizes are just as suitable for the narrower ribbons, particularly the 2mm ribbon. If you use a No. 18 with a 2mm ribbon you will find that the hole made when the shaft of the needle forces the fibres of the fabric apart will be so large in comparison to the ribbon width that the stitch will move around the hole and will not sit firmly in place.

The final choice for needle size is a matter of preference and will be influenced by the width of the ribbon you are using and the ease with which it will draw through the fabric As a rule of thumb and until you gain some experience with the selection of needles for ribbon widths try the following:

Chenille Size 18 - 7mm ribbon and spark organdy
Chenille Size 20 to 22 - 4mm ribbon
Chenille Size 24 - 2mm ribbon

Smaller and finer needles are used when stranded cottons and silks are used to embellish the stitches and designs.

Pin Cushion

I always work with a pin cushion close by, filled with several dozen assorted size chenille and crewel needles suitable for silk ribbon embroidery. When I have used a particular ribbon and there is still a length of it left on the needle I store this in the pin cushion for later use. It may not be used on this project but will often come in handy for the centre of a rose or a single flower on a later project. If you cut the remaining silk ribbon from your needle in order to use the same needle each time you will find that you are left with dozens of pieces of ribbon which you will invariably reject when starting a larger flower. By storing leftover ribbons in this manner you will waste less ribbon.

Scissors

A small sharp pair of embroidery scissors are a must. Tie a piece of ribbon on them or decorate them with a tassel to make them easy to find amongst your work.

Embroidery Hoop

I have found that an embroidery hoop is essential when working with silk ribbon in order to maintain the correct tension on your work. I have several in assorted sizes and they are a standard circular hoop available in most needlework or craft shops. Ensure that the hoop you are using has no splinters poking out from the sides as these will catch your silk ribbon and damage it. You must also be able to adjust your hoop with the tightening mechanism so that your fabric is 'drum' tight. If your hoop is too loose then wrap the inner circle with cotton tape. This will increase the diameter of the inner circle and allow sufficient adjustment of the hoop for you to obtain the tension required. Generally the size of the hoop is governed by the size of the work. The garden landscapes are done in a 300mm (12") hoop and once the fabric is fitted in the hoop it is left in until the work is completed. The smaller hoops are equally suitable for some of the other projects shown, such as the barrettes or perhaps a brooch.

Marking your fabric, placement guides

A water erasable pen can be used to indicate placement guides for stems and flower centres. If you are using one of these always use it as lightly as possible and make the minimum mark on your fabric. A cotton bud dipped in cold water and rubbed gently on the pen mark is all that is required to remove any visible marks from your completed embroidery. Stubborn marks may need to have the process repeated. It is always best to remove the marks as soon as the flower or bush is completed rather than leave this to the end of the project.

A light pencil mark is usually all that is required to indicate the position of any feature in the garden landscapes. This is covered by embroidering over the outlines so ensure that the line is fine enough that your stitching will cover it completely.

Subtle details have been added, upon completion, to some of the garden landscapes using a brown 'Pygma' pen, a waterproof pen available in a variety of colours.

Threads

I have used a variety of threads for the projects in this book.

DMC stranded cottons are very useful and available in an enormous variety of colours. Normally these are chosen to work stems, etc. so it is a simple process to choose one that is close in colour to the silk ribbon to be used.

Kanagawa (1000) Silk Thread is a lovely thread to work with. It is equivalent to approximately three strands of stranded cotton and I find it useful to work the centres of flowers and work background foliage, flowers, trees, etc. in the garden landscapes, generally the softer and lighter shades are used here. It has a lovely sheen to it and provides a luminous look to your finished work.

Rajmahal Art Silk is a stranded silk thread available in a range of 60 colours and has a rich and lustrous sheen to it. I find it compliments the silk ribbon very well although it needs to be worked in short lengths particularly if only one strand is to be used for very fine work.

Madeira sewing threads are used when gold or silver highlights are added to a piece, for example, the spider webs. They are very fine threads most often used for machine embroidery but are useful when fine details are to be added as a final highlight.

DMC metallic thread, a three strand metal thread can also be stranded down to one thread and used here in place of the Madeira threads.

A final word on threads — don't restrict yourself to the above, there are some wonderful threads available and they can add extra dimensions to your work so experiment with them and find ones that you enjoy working with or that help you achieve the look and texture that you are working towards.

Ribbons

Embroidery ribbons are available in both rayon and pure silk. They are now being manufactured in a large variety of stunning colours. The pure silk ribbons are available in a much greater variety of colours and widths than the rayon ribbon. Pure silk is available in 2mm, 4mm, 7mm, 13mm and 32mm although only the 4mm ribbon is available in the full range of 185 colours.

I prefer to work in pure silk ribbon and embellish with pure silk threads but the choice is yours.

Spark organdy ribbon is also used in the garden landscapes. It is particularly useful to fill in large areas without becoming too dense and heavy. This ribbon has a slight sparkle to it and is transparent which allows you to see through it to other stitching and details. It does become distressed easily when embroidering but often this will enhance the embroidery, imitating leaf veins etc. in your work. Once again it needs to be worked in short lengths only. It is currently available in 30 colours and 4 different widths.

All your embroidery ribbons and threads should be stored neatly and carefully to ensure that they are not damaged prior to commencing your project. A neat and easily accessible selection of ribbons and threads will make your embroidery far more enjoyable.

Several methods are successful for storing ribbons

a Wind the ribbons onto empty sewing cotton reels.

b Use an embroidery floss storage card, but this method may require the ribbon to be ironed before use to remove creases.

c Make your own ribbon storage card from thick cardboard from the template as illustrated.

Cut as many as required from thick cardboard. The slots

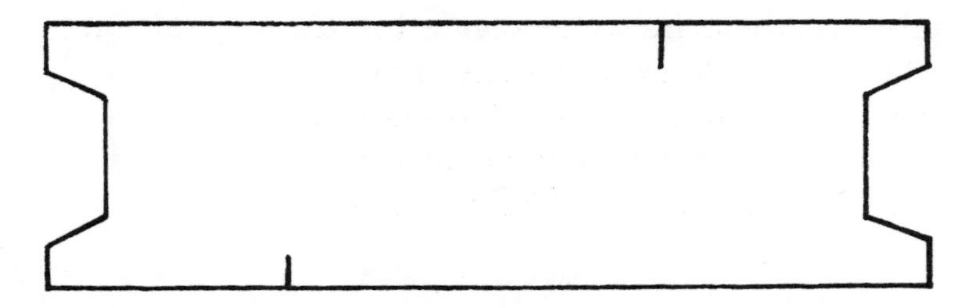

on either side allow you to anchor the end of the ribbon to prevent it unravelling.

d Use a cardboard cylinder with a slit cut into it to accept the end of the ribbon and prevent it from unravelling. With this method several shades of the same colour can be stored together on the one cylinder allowing you to find shades of one colour more easily.

Getting Started

Fit your fabric into your hoop, ensuring that it is 'drum' tight. Cut your ribbon to length, always at an angle. The ribbon should be no longer than 300mm (12").

Thread the needle, following the steps as listed below and the illustration as shown.

1 Thread ribbon through the eye of the needle.

2 Approximately 5mm from the end, loop the ribbon over the point of the needle.

3 Gently pull the free end of the ribbon, this will pull the looped end of the ribbon down the shaft of the needle and lock it over the eye of the needle.

4 Tie a knot in the free end of the ribbon.

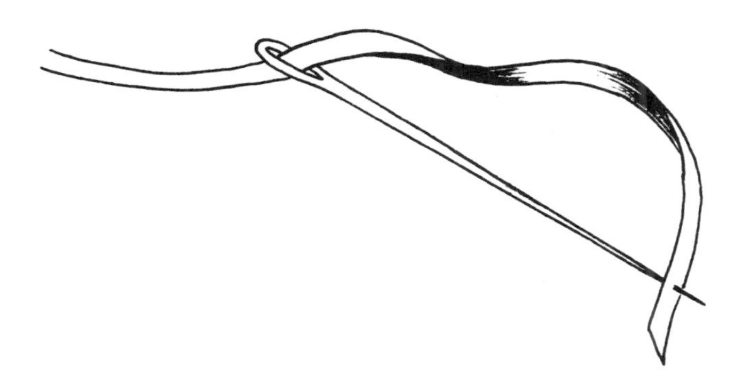

By threading the needle in this manner you will be able to drop the needle at the back of the work, allowing you to use both hands to manipulate the ribbon should it become twisted or to do some stitching in another colour or thread before continuing.

To end off a tail of ribbon after embroidering, simply thread it under the stitches already in place. On a garment or heavy-wear article you may like to take a small stitch in stranded cotton or silk thread over this ribbon tail to ensure that it is caught in place. With the garden landscapes in this book it will be sufficient to thread the end through the back of some already completed stitches.

To rethread a needle once you have used all the ribbon, you will need to cut off the old ribbon to clear the eye for the new length.

The Stitches

Many of the stitches used in ribbon embroidery are formed in the same way as similar stitches for stranded cotton embroidery, with one exception. Ribbon stitch and the variations to this stitch have been developed specially.

If you have a basic understanding of these traditional embroidery stitches then you will have no trouble in interpreting the designs on the projects contained in this book.

Basic ribbon stitch is the most common stitch that I use and it is worthwhile to take the time to practise this stitch before attempting a project.

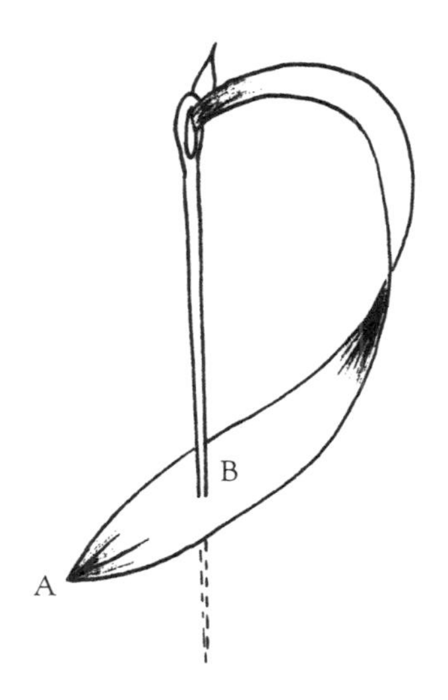

Basic Ribbon Stitch

1 Pull the ribbon through the fabric at A.

2 Ensure that the ribbon is lying flat on your fabric. You may need to use the shaft of your needle to run down the length of the ribbon to discourage and remove any folding.

3 Put the point of the needle back through the middle of the ribbon about 8-10mm from the start of the stitch at B.

4 Pull the needle through the ribbon and fabric and continue to pull until the edges of the ribbon curl in at the tip to form a neat point.

5 Move onto the beginning of your next stitch, or fasten off.

Note: Care must be taken not to pull the ribbon too far towards the end of the stitch formation or this will cause the ribbon to fold in on itself and the full effect of the ribbon width will be lost. You may find it useful to put your thumb or fingernail over the stitch as you pull the ribbon to ensure that it is not pulled too far.

It is easy to vary the effects created with this simple stitch by adjusting the length and tension of the ribbon before piercing with the needle.

Modified Ribbon Stitch

Begin the stitch as you would for basic ribbon stitch. As you pull the needle and ribbon through to the back of the work only pull it so far that a flat end is formed — stop before the ribbon makes a sharp point.

Extended Ribbon Stitch

This is formed in the same way as basic ribbon stitch but the stitch is much longer, anything up to 10cm. On an item of heavy-wear, a fine row of stitching can be worked down the centre of the stitch, if desired. This imitates the central vein of a leaf and it also ensures the stitch remains in place and does not get caught after the article is complete.

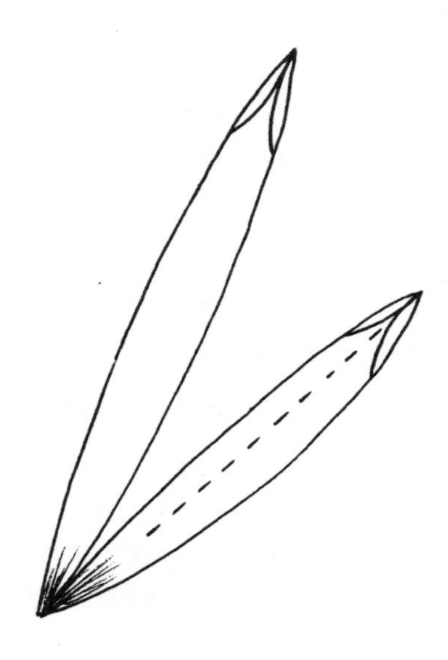

Couched Ribbon Stitch

Basic ribbon stitch is commenced at A. Ribbon is held flat to the fabric at required position and length. (Once again this can be quite long.) Next, 2-3 small stitches in stranded cotton are taken across the width of the ribbon at B, the position of the dotted line. Ribbon is then folded over these stitches, covering them completely. Ribbon stitch is completed at C.

This stitch may also have the vein detail added, as described above, if it is being worked on an item of heavy-wear.

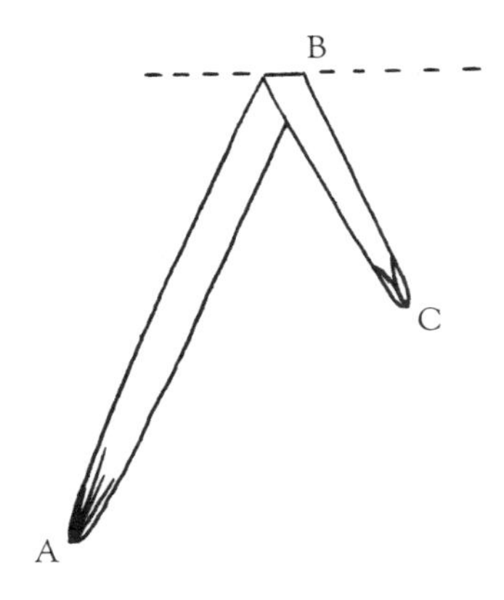

Twisted Ribbon Stitch

Formed as for basic ribbon stitch but before the stitch is completed ribbon is twisted 180 degrees to form the permanent twist in the stitch. Stitch is then completed as normal with a neat point to the end.

This is a useful stitch in the garden landscapes to create variety and the impression of movement.

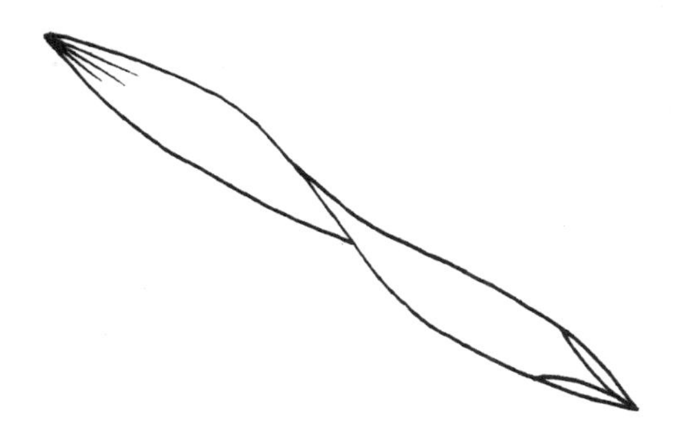

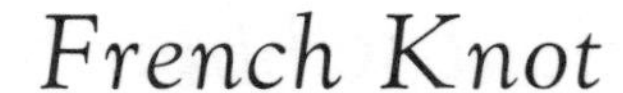

French Knot

1 Pull the ribbon or thread through the fabric at A.

2 Twist the ribbon around the needle once and put the needle back through the fabric at B, as close to A as possible but not into it.

3 Pull the twisted ribbon around the needle until it is quite firm but not so tight that it prevents you pulling the needle through the fabric.

4 Pull the needle through to the back of the fabric.

5 The ribbon will have formed a knot on the top of the fabric.

6 Fasten off, or move to the next stitch.

Note: The size of the knot can be varied by any of the following means:

a Altering the tension of the twist of ribbon around the needle before it is pulled through the fabric, i.e., loose tension will result in a larger knot;

b Wrapping the ribbon or thread around the needle more than once, i e., each successive twist before the needle is pulled through the fabric will increase the size of the knot;

c Changing the width of the ribbon and the size of the needle.

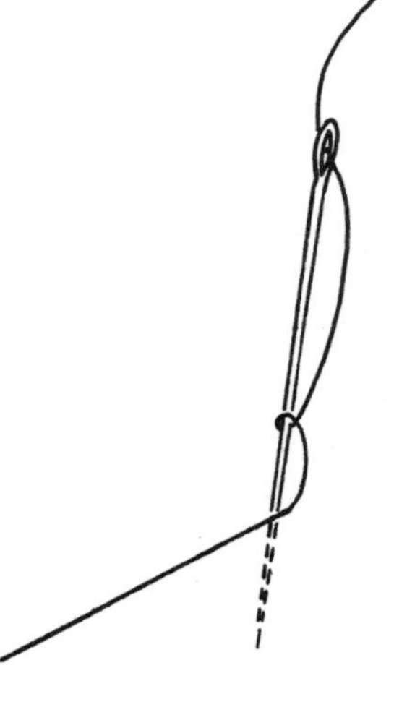

Pistil Stitch

This stitch is formed in the same way as a French knot, but instead of inserting the needle very close to where it emerged through the fabric it is inserted at the distance required for the length of the stitch.

Note: This stitch is usually formed with stranded silk or cotton to form centre details or stamens on flowers. The thread can be wrapped around the needle once, twice or more depending on the size of the knot required.

Feather Stitch

Bring the needle through the fabric at A, go down at B and emerge at C. The next stage of the stitch are these steps reversed to the other side.

Stitches are worked alternatively from one side to the other. I use this stitch to form the delicate foliage effects, usually in silver or gold threads, but occasionally in cotton or silk on some of the projects. It is also useful to 'fill' in a space and balance a design without creating a bulky effect.

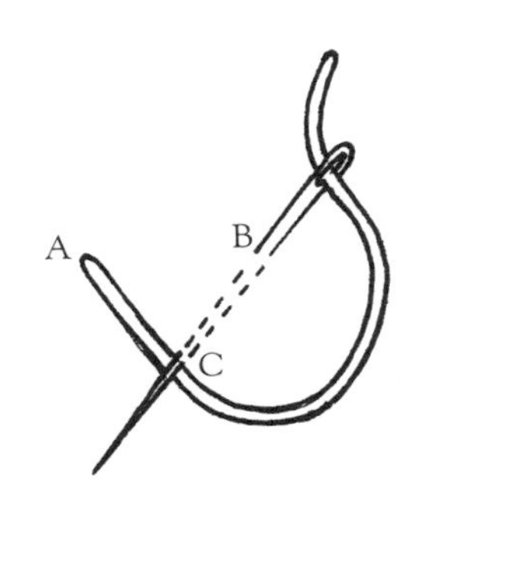

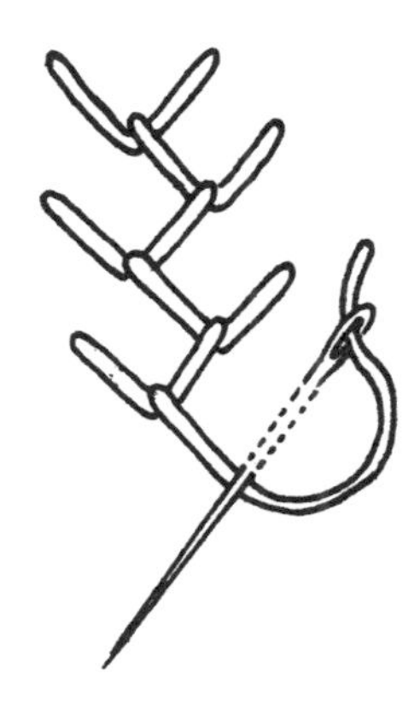

Stem Stitch

This stitch is formed (usually in stranded cotton or silk) by coming up at A, going through the fabric at B and reemerging at C.

This stitch can be varied by the length of the stitch taken and the number of threads used.

Note: Almost all of the branches and stems in the garden landscapes are formed using this stitch. To create heavier stems you can work two rows of stem stitch side by side.

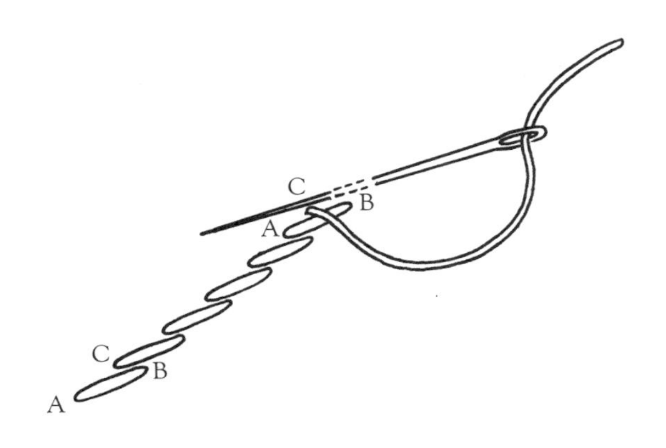

Loop Stitch

1 Bring ribbon through the fabric, ensuring it is laying as flat as possible with no twists in it.

2 Turn it back on itself 180 degrees and reinsert needle immediately above the beginning of the stitch.

3 Pull needle until the 'loop' is the desired length. Use your thumb to encourage loop to lay flat until the ribbon is secured at the back.

Lazy Daisy Stitch

1 Bring the ribbon up at A and form a loop.

2 Go down at B, quite close to A and emerge at C.

3 Take the ribbon through to the back of the work at D and form a small stitch to anchor the loop in place.

Note: This stitch is used in conjunction with a straight stitch to form an iris flower.

It is important to keep the ribbons flat as each stitch is formed.

To complete the straight stitch to form the iris flower bring the needle up at E, thread it through the base of the completed lazy daisy stitch and then take the needle through to the back of the work at F. Manipulate the ribbon to keep it flat as you complete this stitch.

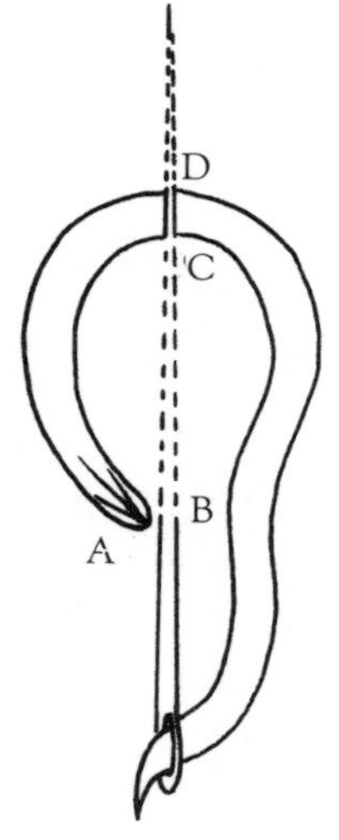

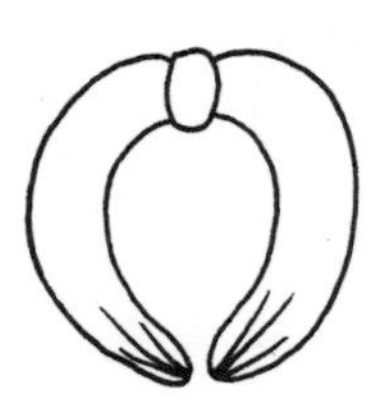

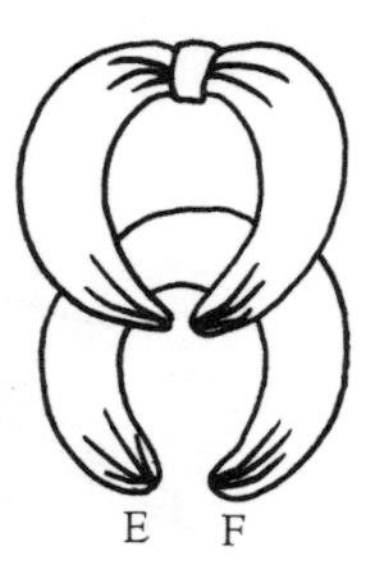

Fly Stitch

1 Bring thread through fabric at A.

2 Reinsert at B, emerge at C.

3 The resulting 'V' stitch is held in place by reinserting the needle to form a small holding stitch. This holding stitch can be made longer if required.

Note: This stitch is most often used on buds to add detail and to anchor them to the foliage or stems.

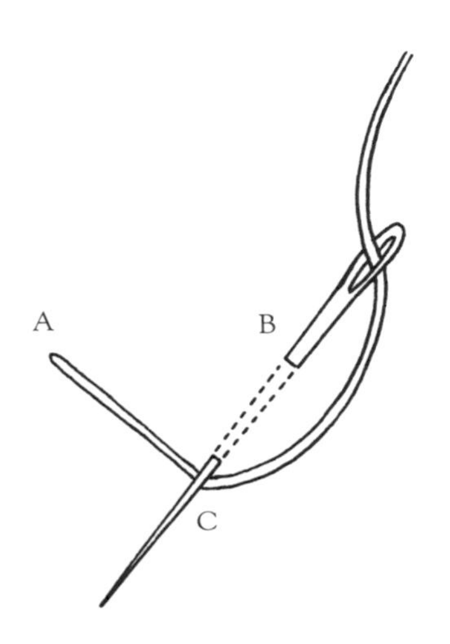

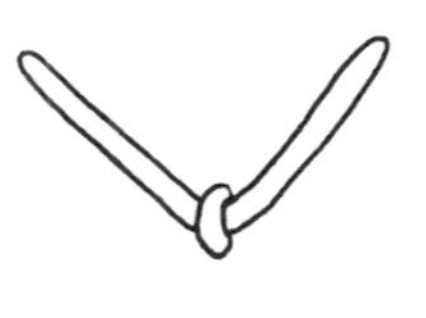

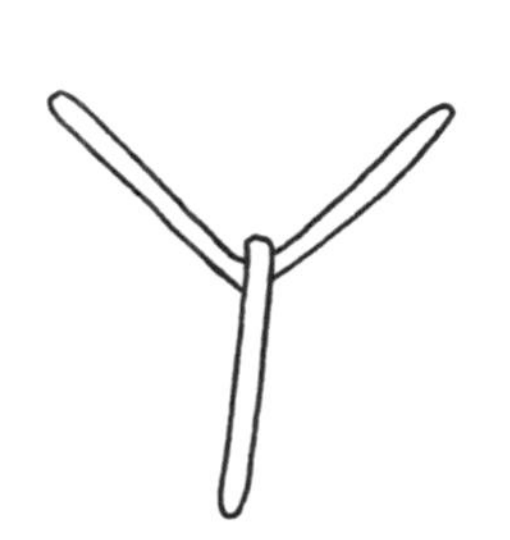

Straight Stitch

1 Emerge through fabric at A, ensure ribbon is laying as flat as possible.

2 Reinsert at B.

3 Fasten off at back of work or work next stitch.

Note: This stitch is most often worked in stranded cotton and in combination with fly stitch to add details to flower buds.

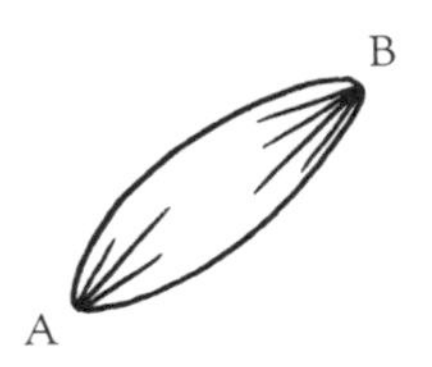

Spider Web Rose

1 Form the spokes of the web with 2 strands of cotton in a fly stitch with an extended tail to form a 'Y'

2 Form straight stitches, D-E and F-E. Ensure all stitches are evenly spaced. Only 5 spokes are required.

3 Bring ribbon up at E, the centre of the spokes. Reverse the needle and weave the eye of the needle under and over the alternating spokes until all the spokes are covered. (By weaving with the eye of the needle instead of the point you will ensure that the point of the needle does not catch and pull ribbon that is already woven into place.)

4 Allow the ribbon to twist and keep it quite loose as you work.

5 Return ribbon to the back of the work, through the fabric, and fasten off.

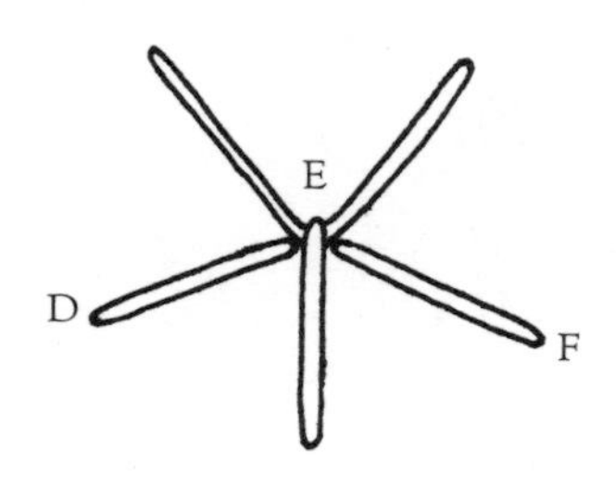

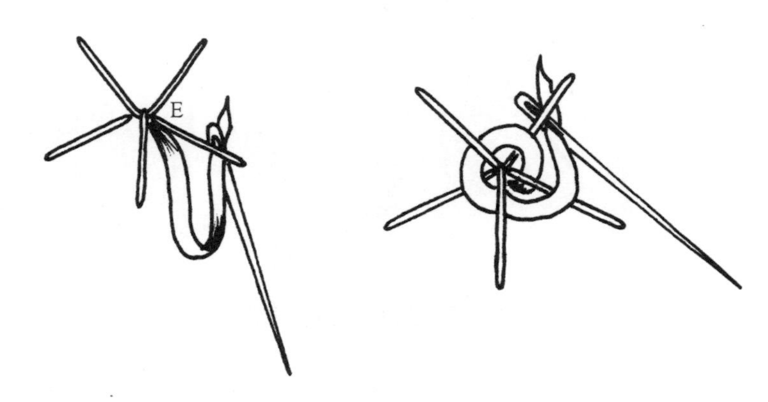

Note: Spider web spokes should be worked in a colour to match the ribbon that will be used to form the rose.

By allowing the ribbon to twist as you weave you will create a more natural looking rose. Don't pull the ribbon too tight as this will make the rose look bulky and it won't sit close to the fabric.

The size of the rose can be varied by the initial size of the web, the width of the ribbon used, the number of times the ribbon is woven around the spokes and the tension of the ribbon as it is woven.

A French knot in a darker shade may be worked first at the centre of the spokes to form the centre of the rose. For a larger rose a triangle of French knots may be worked at the centre.

Formation of Flower Buds

Flower buds and partially-opened flowers are formed using a combination of three stitches in both ribbon and stranded threads. The size of the bud formed is determined by the number of ribbon stitches worked together.

1 A single bud = 1 ribbon stitch + 1 fly stitch + 1 straight stitch.

2 A larger bud = 2 ribbon stitches + 1 fly stitch + 2 straight stitches.

3 A partially opened flower = 3 ribbon stitches + 1 fly stitch + 3 straight stitches.

Buds are formed using the basic ribbon stitch in the desired colour. A fly stitch and a straight stitch are formed over this ribbon stitch as illustrated. An extra straight stitch is formed over each extra ribbon stitch included in the bud formation.

Both the straight stitch and the fly stitch are formed in stranded cotton to match whatever colour the stem or branch of the flower has been worked in.

Formation of the Spider Web

Very early one morning I noticed on a clump of fern that grows in my garden about 50 tiny, perfect spider webs. The image of those webs stayed with me all day. That evening I was working on one of the garden landscapes and decided to place a web, complete with a tiny spider, among the flowers. The tiny web has now become somewhat of a trademark of my work and both students and friends look for it when they study a newly completed piece. As I also make patchwork quilts and do wool embroidery it appears on several quilts and blankets as well. Placed on a floral print or amongst the colourful wool flowers it doesn't appear obvious to many but I have found that it has become a unique way to personalise each individual project.

The addition of the spider web may not always be appropriate; for example, you may not want them on the hair barrettes or the brooches, but can be included on the larger projects to lend a little individuality and sense of fun to your work. Directions for creating your own spider web are included or you may, with the help of a little imagination, like to create a distinctive 'trademark' of your own.

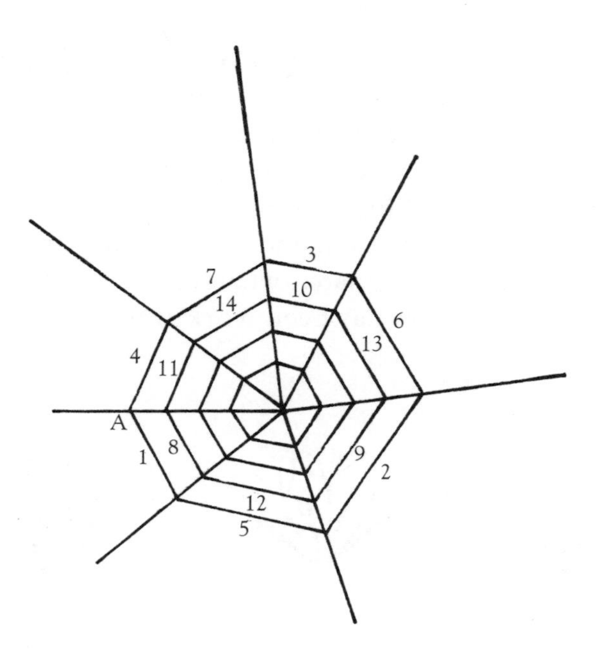

Directions

I use Madeira metallic machine sewing thread to create the webs, either in silver or gold. The spokes of the web are formed first, in straight stitch and always an uneven number. They are anchored to the flowers simply by stitching close to the leaf, bud, etc. The web is then formed by taking straight stitches, working from the outside to the centre between every alternate spoke in each round. It will take you 2 rounds of stitching between the spokes to complete 1 round of web. By working in this manner you will be able to put tension on the thread of the web as you create it and not pull the spokes unevenly by stitching over them.

Once you have completed this outside ring, move a little further in and complete a second round, third round, etc. It usually takes 4-5 rounds to complete the entire web.

The spider is simply formed by stitching a single wrap French knot using one strand of thread over one of the spokes.

Selecting Colours

Many people comment on the realistic effects created in the garden landscapes and also the degree of depth there is in each embroidery.

This effect is not only a result of the inclusion of painted backgrounds, which add dimension, but the careful choice of the colours for each individual bush and flower.

I am very fortunate that our home is surrounded by a lovely garden, and there is a huge variety of plants, trees, ferns and bulbs for me to study. Quite often while working in the garden I will be inspired to recreate in embroidery a particular flower or bush. It also allows me the opportunity to match a ribbon exactly to the plant that I am embroidering.

I keep a little notebook in my work box which has the ribbon colour and number closest to a particular flower in the garden. I always note them down as I match them. And, because the garden is a seasonal garden and many bulbs are dormant for most of the year and other plants and bushes only flower once a year this notebook becomes a handy reference when I am trying to recreate them in a landscape after their flowering season has finished.

Other sources of inspiration for flower colours and types are garden nurseries where you can wander among the huge variety of plants and flowering bushes. Plant and seed catalogues too are a wonderful source as they generally have colour photographs of a type of plant and then all the hybrid colour variations available. Public gardens and the gardens of friends and neighbours can also be utilised.

Indeed you will get to a point where you will become acutely aware of colours that will adapt well to an embroidered landscape, and flowers that are easy to interpret with ribbon and thread.

Don't be frightened to substitute colours if you don't have a particular thread or colour. In many instances this is a lovely way to personalise a design and make it your own. Don't feel that you have to adhere strictly to the colours recommended in the charts accompanying the flower designs in this book. They are included as a guide only.

You may have a favourite flower that you wish to feature or even a part of your garden or the garden of a friend that you wish to capture on fabric. Match up several ribbons to flower colours and then sit down and enjoy the creative process. You may also have a favourite piece of fabric that you wish to use which may require a change of ribbon colours to do it justice.

If you don't have the thread or ribbon listed and access to it is difficult, then substitute. The colour description should help you find a ribbon which when used in conjunction with a variety of other colours will give a very satisfactory result when the whole is blended to form a landscape. Likewise if your DMC thread collection does not include the colour listed but you have a thread that is close in colour and tones well with the silk ribbon you have chosen then use it.

Eventually you will begin to get a feel for putting colours together and you will begin to embroider by colour rather than by number. You will be able to recall the colour of a flower or bush that you wish to recreate in your work and you will be able to select, from memory, the ribbon and corresponding thread before you begin. At this stage you will find that you will attain a real flow to your work, creativity will take over and you will be able to achieve very rewarding results.

The Greens

I have included here a list of the variety of 'green' silk ribbons that I use in my work on a regular basis. They range from a light grey green to a very rich and dark forest green. The chart will be useful to you when you are matching threads to silk ribbon for the stems and leaves of the landscapes and other projects.

I have found that for the landscapes, or indeed any floral embroidery, to be successful and attain a degree of realism, it is important to incorporate as many shades of green as possible.

In the list I have given the corresponding colour for

DMC stranded cotton and Rajmahal Art Silk along with a personal description of the shade of green for your reference. Because of the more limited number of colours available in the Rajmahal range it is more difficult to accurately match thread and silk colours. However if you want all your work to be embroidered using pure silk threads then it may be worth the effort in searching out stockists to obtain the threads required. The lustre of these threads will make the effort worthwhile.

Rajmahal stranded threads need to be worked using short lengths only. Often you will be working with only one strand of pure silk and if worked in longer lengths than 30cm it will become distressed and fray, but, as already mentioned it is worth the challenge.

DMC threads are the easiest to obtain and are easy to work with. If you have a DMC thread in a colour that compliments the silk you are going to use, but it is not the exact shade listed below, then use what you have. The list below is meant to be a guide only.

A combination of stranded silk threads and stranded cotton threads works equally as well as using one or the other.

No.	2mm	4mm	7mm	Colour Description	DMC	Rajmahal
20	*	*	*	Medium grass green	3346	521
21	*	*	*	Dark forest green	319	65
31	*	*	*	Light apple green	523	802
32	*	*	*	Light blue green	3817	926
33	*	*	*	Medium blue green	520	805
56	*	*	*	Light mustard green	370	311
62		*		Light ice green	369	802
72		*	*	Dark jungle green	937	421
73		*	*	Light grey green	3022	221
74		*	*	Smokey grey green	5028	926
75		*	*	Dark blue green	934	926
143		*		Bronze khaki green	830	311
170		*		Light yellow green	734	521
171		*		Medium olive green	470	521

* Denotes the widths in which the silk ribbon is available.

The Flowers

Following are detailed drawings and instructions for the stitching of each individual flower group. The flower drawings appear in alphabetical order according to their common name or description. If you have any difficulty at this stage in remembering the stitches used to create these flowers please refer to the stitch guides.

The colour reference numbers for both the silk ribbon and the DMC threads for embellishment have been included, along with the stitching instructions. In many instances I have included alternative colours that you may wish to use to create the flowers. As a general rule the foliage colour remains the same if you use the alternative flower colour.

The individual thread reference number as well as the number of strands used and the silk ribbon reference number along with the width of the ribbon has been listed next to each component. If you prefer to use all silk threads as I have done please substitute the Rajmahal Art Silk thread number whenever a DMC cotton thread has been listed by referring to the chart on page 30 which will give you the reference numbers for the greens used. I have given the DMC stranded cotton thread numbers as they are the most common.

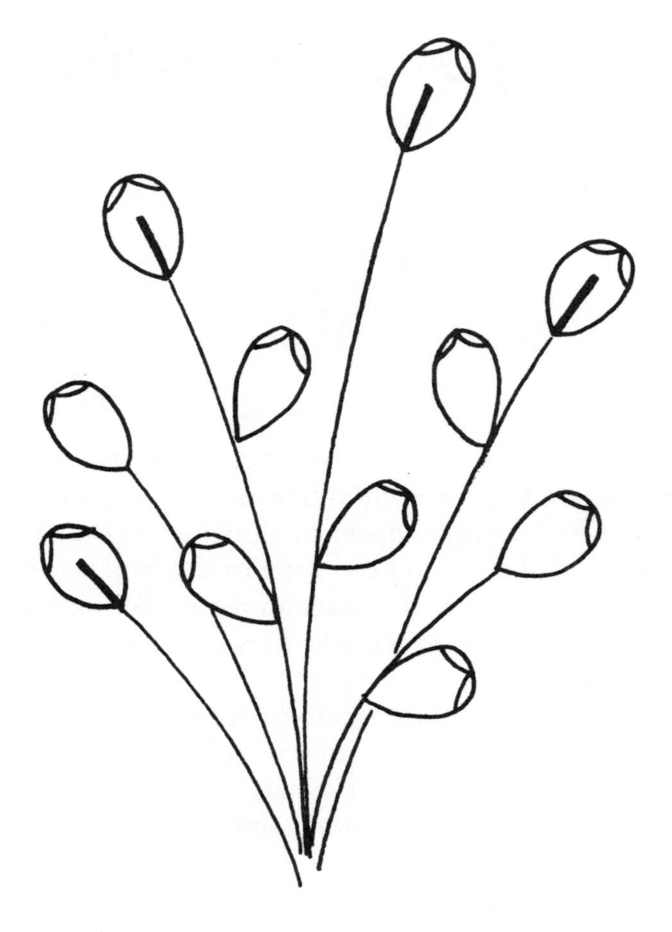

Arum Lilies

	No & Size	Colour Description	Stitch Used
Stem	3346, 1 strand	Medium grass green	Stem
Leaves	20, 7mm	Medium grass green	Ribbon
Flowers	1, 7mm	White	Ribbon
Flower stamen	444, 3 strands	Bright yellow	Straight

Sewing notes: Kanagawa 1000, also in bright yellow, can be used for the large flower stamen, if available.

Order of work: Stems, flowers, flower stamen detail, leaves.

Bluebells

	No & Size	Colour Description	Stitch Used
Stem	319, 1 strand	Dark forest green	Stem
Leaves	21, 2mm	Dark forest green	Extended ribbon
			Couched ribbon
Flower petals	44, 2mm	Medium sky blue	Modified ribbon
Flower details	21, 2mm	Dark forest green	Ribbon

Sewing notes: Calyx detail of flower is formed by adding 2 ribbon stitches over base of stitches that form the flower.

Order of work: Leaves, stems, flowers, flower details.

Daffodils

	No & Size	Colour Description	Stitch Used
Stem	3346,1 strand	Medium grass green	Stem
Leaves	20, 2mm	Medium grass green	Extended ribbon
			Couched ribbon
Flower petals	13, 2mm	Pale lemon	Ribbon
Flower centres	15, 4mm	Bright yellow	Loop
Flower bud	15, 4mm	Bright yellow	Ribbon
Bud detail	3346,1 strand	Medium grass green	Fly & Straight

Sewing notes: For stitches required to add details to flower buds refer to stitch guide; buds are formed in the manner described.

Order of work: Leaves, flower petals, flower centres, buds, bud details, stems.

Daisy (Variation No.1)

	No & Size	Colour Description	Stitch Used
Stem	520, 1 strand	Medium blue green	Stem
Leaves	33, 4mm	Medium blue green	Ribbon
Flower petals	128, 4mm	Raspberry pink	Ribbon
Flower centres	15, 4mm	Bright yellow	French knot
Flower bud	128, 4mm	Raspberry pink	Ribbon stitch
Bud detail	520, 1 strand	Medium blue green	Fly & Straight

Alternative colours

Stem	369, 1 strand	Light ice green
Leaves	62, 4mm	Light ice green
Petals	8, 4mm	Pale pink
Flower centres	13, 4mm	Pale lemon

Sewing notes: Side views of flowers are formed keeping the stitches below the horizontal line across the centre of the flower. It may help to keep a clock face in mind and work the end of the petals at 4,5,6,7 and 8 o'clock. Leave a small circle of clear space in the middle of the petals to work the flower centre. In this way the petals will not be pulled as you work the centre. I have given an alternative list of colours but any combination generally works with this flower.

Order of work: Stems, flower petals, buds, flower centres, bud details.

Daisy (Variation No.2)

	No & Size	Colour Description	Stitch Used
Stem	3346, 1 strand	Medium grass green	Stem
Leaves	20, 4mm	Medium grass green	Extended ribbon Couched ribbon
Flower petals	1, 4mm	Antique white	Ribbon
Flower centres	15, 4mm	Bright yellow	Ribbon
Flower bud	1, 4mm	Antique white	Ribbon
Bud detail	3346,1 strand	Medium grass green	Fly & Straight

Alternative colours

Stem	937, 1 strand	Dark jungle green
Leaves	72, 4mm	Dark jungle green
Petals	158, 4mm	Medium dusky pink
Flower centres	13, 4mm	Pale lemon

Sewing notes: As for Variation 1, all petals for the side view of the flowers are kept below the horizontal line. As the full daisies are worked keep the top petals slightly shorter than the lower petals.

Order of work: Leaves, flowers, buds, flower centres, bud details, stems.

Flowering Tree or Shrub

Ribbon — Colour used depends on the type of shrub you are creating and where work is to appear, generally the darker colours are worked in the foreground, lighter tones in the background.

Thread — Select a colour to tone with desired silk ribbon.

	No & Size	**Colour Description**	**Stitch Used**
Stem	1 strand	As selected	Stem
Leaves	2mm or 4mm	As selected	Ribbon
Flowers	2mm or 4mm	As selected	French knot

Sewing notes: This is a useful addition to the garden landscapes as it will give you the opportunity to repeat a colour or tone to achieve a balanced composition without creating a particular plant. It is also useful to fill in areas that you need to blend into the background. To achieve a realistic effect, choose colours to represent the plant you are trying to recreate. For example, Diosma, wattle, native dog rose, yellow broom, tea tree, flowering fruit trees, etc.

Order of work: Stem, leaves, flowers.

Foliage

Ribbon — Select a light coloured ribbon, eg. light brown, beige, pale green. Pale coloured spark organdy works very well when used to create the leaves for this foliage.

Thread — Select a colour to tone with desired silk ribbon.

	No & Size	**Colour Description**	**Stitch Used**
Stem	1 strand	As selected	Stem
Leaves	2mm or 4mm	As selected	Ribbon

Sewing notes: Variations to this useful fill in stitch can be easily achieved by using different width silks, a combination of silk and organdy ribbon in similar colours or complementary colours worked alternatively along the branch.

Order of work: Stem, leaves.

Forget Me Knot

	No & Size	Colour Description	Stitch Used
Flower centres	15, 4mm	Bright yellow	French knot
Flower petals	125, 4mm	Light blue	French knot
Leaves	31, 2mm	Light apple green	Ribbon

Sewing notes: Size of completed flower may be altered by using 2mm ribbon in the selected colours instead of 4mm. This will create smaller flowers. Less tension while using the 4mm ribbon will form a slightly larger flower.

Order of work: Flower centres, flower petals, 5 or 6 as needed to complete a circle around the centre, leaves.

Foxglove

	No & Size	Colour Description	Stitch Used
Stem	520, 1 strand	Medium blue green	Stem
Flower buds	124, 4mm	Very pale blue	French knot
	125, 4mm	Light blue	French knot

Flowers	124, 4mm	Very pale blue	Ribbon
	125, 4mm	Light blue	Ribbon
Leaves	33, 4mm	Medium blue green	Extended ribbon

Sewing notes: Work the flower from the top to the base as this is the most economical way of working the ribbon. The French knots at the top of the stalk are worked before commencing the flowers.

Order of work: Stem, flower buds, flowers, leaves.

Gerbera

	No & Size	Colour Description	Stitch Used
Stem	319,1 strand	Dark forest green	Stem
Leaves	21, 2mm	Dark forest green	Ribbon
Flower centres	15, 4mm	Bright yellow	French knot
Flower petals	128, 2mm	Raspberry pink	Ribbon
Flower buds	128, 2mm	Raspberry pink	Ribbon
Bud detail	319,1 strand	Dark forest green	Fly & Straight

Sewing notes: Leaves are kept close together as they are worked side by side up the stem. Petals for flowers are kept below the horizontal line to give only the side view of the flower.

Order of work: Stem, leaves, flower centres, flower petals, buds, bud details.

Geranium

	No & Size	Colour Description	Stitch Used
Stem	319,1 strand	Dark forest green	Stem
Leaves	21, 4mm	Dark forest green	Straight, 2 of
Flowers	50, 4mm	Rich deep red	French knots

Sewing notes: Straight stitches for leaves are worked very close together. Flowers are French knots grouped together in a small circle.

Order of work: Stem, leaves, flower heads.

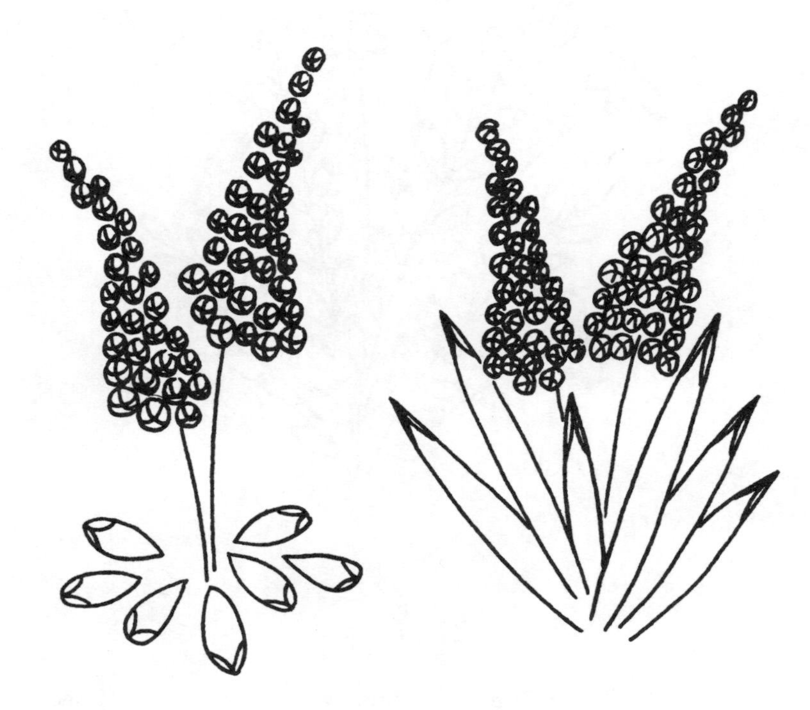

Grape Hyacinths

	No & Size	Colour Description	Stitch Used
Stem	470,1 strand	Medium olive green	Stem
Leaves	171, 4mm	Medium olive green	Ribbon
Flowers	102, 4mm	Deep mauve	French knots

Sewing notes: For the alternative leaf detail as illustrated, extended ribbon stitch may be used to create a different effect. Twisted ribbon stitch can also be used with this flower. The French knots are formed in an elongated triangle, slightly curved, to create the flower head.

Order of Work: Stem, leaves, flower head.

Iris (Variation No. 1)

	No & Size	Colour Description	Stitch Used
Stem	520, 1 strand	Medium blue green	Stem
Leaves	33, 4mm	Medium blue green	Extended ribbon Couched ribbon
Flowers	13, 4mm	Pale lemon	Chain & Straight
Flower buds	13, 4mm	Pale lemon	Ribbon
Bud details	520, 1 strand	Medium blue green	Fly & Straight

Sewing notes: Work the leaves first and then position the flowers over the top of and between these. To form the iris refer to details under the stitch guide for lazy daisy stitch.

Order of work: Leaves, flowers, buds, bud details, stems.

Iris (Variation No. 2)

	No & Size	Colour Description	Stitch Used
Stem	520, 1 strand	Medium blue green	Stem
Leaves	33, 4mm	Medium blue green	Extended ribbon Couched ribbon
Flowers	179, 4mm	Medium grape	Ribbon
Flower buds	179, 4mm	Medium grape	Ribbon
Bud details	520, 1 strand	Medium blue green	Fly & Straight
Flower details	744, 1 strand	Medium yellow	Straight

Sewing notes: As for Variation No. 1, the leaves are worked first. Flowers are then formed using 5 ribbon stitches, 2 upper and 3 lower stitches. Ensure that the lower stitches are slightly longer than the upper ones. The straight stitches in stranded cotton are added last. This flower can be worked in almost any colour but the leaves remain the same medium blue green.

Order of Work: Leaves, flowers, buds, bud details and flower details.

Lavender

	No & Size	Colour Description	Stitch Used
Stem	520, 1 strand	Medium blue green	Stem
Leaves	33, 2mm	Medium blue green	Ribbon
Flowers	23, 4mm	Deep mauve	French knots

Sewing notes: Make a very slight curve in the stems as they are worked; continue the line of this curve as you work the flower head in the French knots.

Order of work: Stems, leaves, flower heads.

Lily of the Valley

	No & Size	Colour Description	Stitch Used
Stem	3346, 1 strand	Medium grass green	Stem
Leaves	20, 4mm	Medium grass green	Extended ribbon
Flowers	3, 4mm	White	French knots

Sewing notes: Work the stems with a slight curve in them. French knots, representing the flowers are evenly spaced along the end of this curved stem.

Order of work: Leaves, stems, flowers.

Magnolia

	No & Size	Colour Description	Stitch Used
Stem	470, 1 strand	Medium olive green	Stem
Lower petals	50, 4mm	Rich deep red	Ribbon
Upper petals	4, 4mm	Very pale pink	Ribbon
Leaves	171, 4mm	Medium olive green	Ribbon

Sewing notes: The magnolia flowers are worked in two stages. The dark red stitches are worked first, then the pale pink stitches worked over the top of these. The flowers appear in two sizes, with three or five petals. The dark red petals are shown shaded on the illustration. The leaves are added quite thickly after the flowers are formed.

Order of work: Stem, lower flower petals, upper flower petals, leaves.

Pansy

	No & Size	Colour Description	Stitch Used
Stem	3346, 1 strand	Medium grass green	Straight
Outer petals	85, 7mm	Deep purple	Ribbon
Inner petals	4, 4mm	Black	Ribbon
Flower centres	15, 4mm	Bright yellow	French knot
Flower bud	85, 7mm	Deep purple	Ribbon
Bud detail	3346, 1 strand	Medium grass green	Fly & Straight
Flower detail	Ecru, 1 strand	Ecru	Straight
Leaf detail	3346, 1 strand	Medium grass green	Straight

Sewing notes: Petals, both inner and outer have one or two straight stitches worked over them at the completion of the flower (see illustration). The leaves also have a straight stitch detail. Buds are worked with either a single ribbon stitch for a tight bud or 2 ribbon stitches, close together at the base, for a larger more open bud.

Order of work: Flower centre, outer flower petals, inner flower petals, buds, leaves, flower details, bud detail, leaf details.

Rose — Briar or Ground Cover Rose

	No & Size	Colour Description	Stitch Used
Stem	3817, 1 strand	Light blue green	Stem
Leaves	32, 4mm	Light blue green	Ribbon
Flower petals	163, 7mm	Very light rose pink	Ribbon
Flower centres	13, 4mm	Pale lemon	French knot
Flower bud	163, 7mm	Very light rose pink	Ribbon
Flower details	745,1 strand	Medium yellow	Pistil
Bud details	3817, 1 strand	Light blue green	Fly & Straight

Sewing notes: Full flowers are worked with 5 petals around a French knot centre. Pistil stitch in stranded cotton is worked over the flower petals, 2 stitches in each petal to represent stamens. Leaves are worked in groups of 3 or 5.

Order of work: Flower petals, flower centre, flower details, stems, buds, bud details, leaves.

Rose Bush (Hybrid Tea)

	No & Size	Colour Description	Stitch Used
Stem	319, 1 strand	Dark forest green	Stem
Flowers	15, 4mm	Bright yellow	Spider web rose
Flower buds	15, 4mm	Bright yellow	Ribbon
Leaves	21, 4mm	Dark forest green	Ribbon
Bud details	319, 1 strand	Dark forest green	Fly & Straight

Sewing notes: Fully opened roses are positioned on the stems first. Buds formed with either 1, 2 or 3 ribbon stitches depending on the size of the bud required are then positioned on the branches. The ribbon stitches to form these buds are worked very close to one another at the base of the stitch and fan out at the top of the stitch. Leaves are worked in groups of 3 and 5 near the base of the bush and as single leaves near the top of the bush.

Order of work: Stems, full flowers, buds, bud details, leaves.

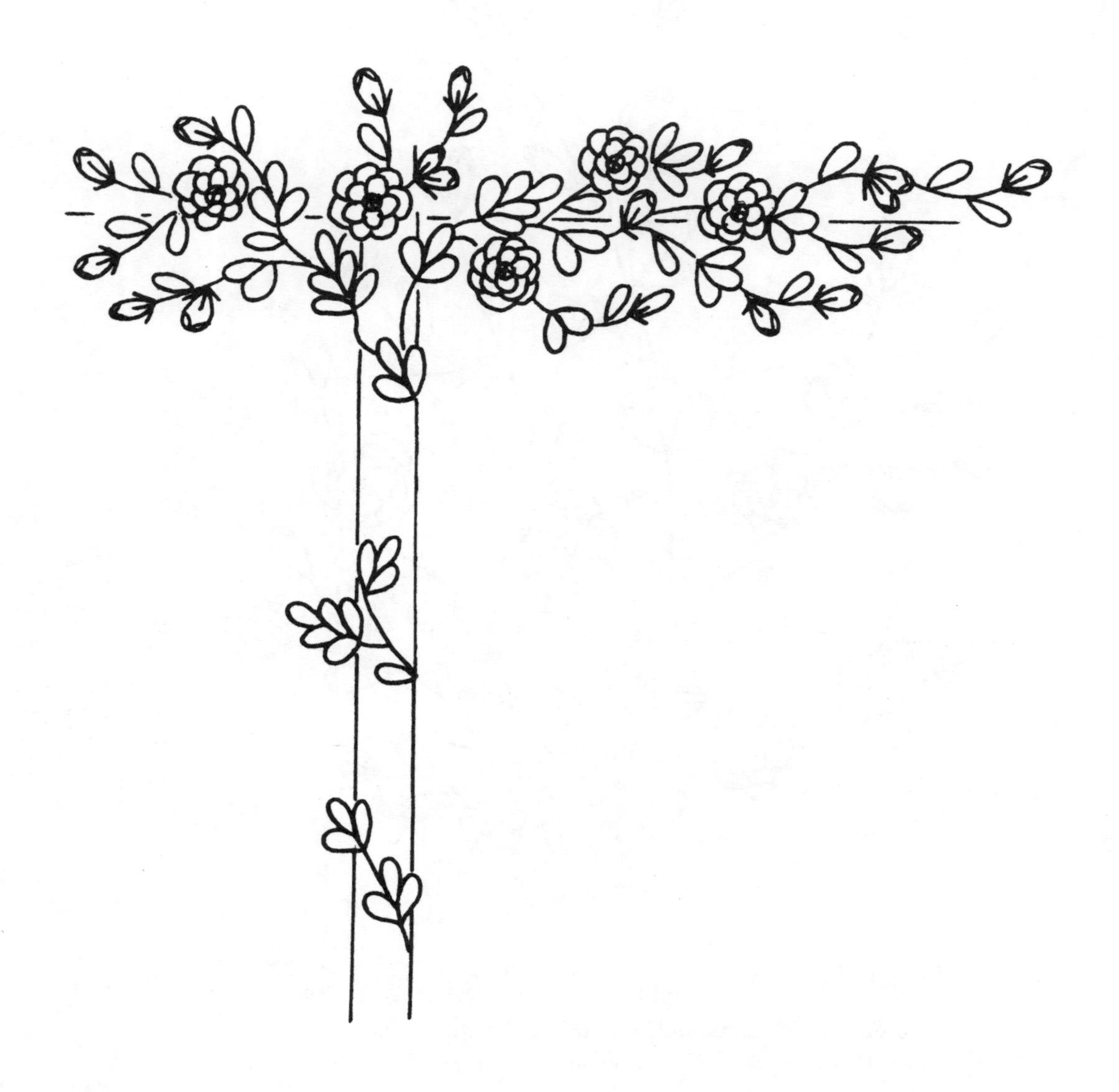

Rose (Climbing)

	No & Size	Colour Description	Stitch Used
Stem	3346, 1 Strand	Medium grass green	Stem
Flowers	14, 4mm	Pale lemon	Spider web rose
Buds	15, 4mm	Pale lemon	Ribbon
Leaves	20, 2mm	Medium grass green	Ribbon
Bud details	3346, 1 strand	Medium grass green	Fly & Straight

Sewing notes: see those for hybrid tea rose bush

Order of work: Stems, full flowers, buds, bud details, leaves.

Rose (Standard)

	No & Size	Colour Description	Stitch Used
Stem	841, 2 strands	Light brown	Stem, 2 rows
Branches	937, 1 strand	Dark jungle green	Stem
Flowers	50, 4mm	Rich dark red	Spider web rose
Buds	50, 4mm	Rich dark red	Ribbon
Bud details	937, 1 strand	Dark jungle green	Fly & Straight
Leaves	72, 4mm	Dark jungle green	Stem

Sewing notes: Generally formed as for the Hybrid tea rose bush.

Order of work: Stem branches, full flowers, buds, bud details, leaves.

Rose (Weeping standard)

	No & Size	Colour Description	Stitch Used
Stem	841, 2 strands	Light brown	Stem, 3 rows
Branches	319, 1 strand	Dark forest green	Stem
Flowers	8, 4mm	Pale pink	Spider web rose
Buds	8, 4mm	Pale pink	Ribbon
Bud details	319, 1 strand	Dark forest green	Fly & Straight
Leaves	21, 2mm	Dark forest green	Ribbon

Sewing notes: Generally formed as for Hybrid tea rose bush. If desired some of the leaves may be formed with spark organdy ribbon in a complimentary colour.

Shade 32 in either 5mm or 9mm widths works well with silk No. 21.

Order of work: Stem, branches, full flowers, buds, bud details and leaves.

Snowdrops

	No & Size	Colour Description	Stitch Used
Stems	319, 1 strand	Dark forest green	Stem
Leaves	21, 4mm	Dark forest green	Extended ribbon Couched ribbon
Flowers	1, 2mm	Antique white	Ribbon stitch
Flower detail	319, 1 strand	Dark forest green	French knot

Sewing notes: Flowers are formed by placing two ribbon stitches very close together at the base and fanning the ends out slightly. The detail is added to these two stitches by working a single wrap French knot at the end of each ribbon stitch as illustrated.

Order of work: Leaves, stems, flower petals, flower details.

Violets

	No & Size	Colour Description	Stitch Used
Stem	3346, 1 strand	Medium grass green	Straight
Flower petals	84, 4mm	Purple	Ribbon
Flower centre	15, 4mm	Bright yellow	French knot
Flower bud	84, 4mm	Purple	Ribbon
Bud detail	3346, 1 strand	Medium grass green	Fly & Straight
Leaves	20, 4mm	Medium grass green	Ribbon

Sewing notes: Form the lower petals first with the centre petal slightly longer than the outer petals. The upper petals are much shorter than the lower ones.

Order of work: Flower petals, flower centre, bud, bud details and leaves.

Wisteria

	No & Size	Colour Description	Stitch Used
Stem	3346, 2 strands	Medium grass green	Stem
Branches	3346, 1 strand	Medium grass green	Stem
Flower clusters	101 & 102, 4mm	Light & deep mauve	French knots
Leaves	20, 4mm	Medium grass green	Ribbon

Sewing notes: Leaves are generally worked in groups of 3 and 5. They are formed as single leaves towards the end of the branches. Flower clusters are formed in triangular groups with the upper French knots worked in the lighter of the two colours used.

Order of work: Stem, branches, flower clusters and leaves.

The Brooches

Four individual designs have been included for these brooches. You may like to design one of your own or change the colours of any of the designs featured. The construction of the brooch, once the embroidery is finished, remains the same.

Posy of Violets

84	4mm	Purple
15	4mm	Bright yellow
171	4mm	Medium olive green
521	1 strand	Rajmahal

Bouquet of Roses

157	4mm	Very light dusky pink
158	4mm	Medium dusky pink
159	4mm	Dark dusky pink
65	2mm	Light caramel
33	2mm	Dark blue green
926	1 strand	Rajmahal
165	1 strand	Rajmahal
802	1 strand	Rajmahal

Madeira metallic thread — gold No. 6

The gold thread is used at the completion of the ribbon embroidery to add fine highlights between the flowers using feather stitch.

Bunch of Daisies

44	2mm	Medium sky blue
15	2mm	Bright yellow
20	2mm	Medium grass green
65	2mm	Light caramel
521	1 strand	Rajmahal

Madeira metallic thread — silver

The silver thread is used once again at the completion of the embroidery as described for the rose design above.

Carpet of Flowers

127	2mm	Light raspberry pink
33	2mm	Dark blue green
3350	3 strands	Deep bright pink (DMC)
13	2mm	Pale lemon
15	2mm	Bright yellow
20	2mm	Medium grass green

3	4mm	White
15	2mm	Bright yellow
170	4mm	Light yellow green
84	2mm	Purple
15	2mm	Bright yellow
5	2mm	Very pale pink
3711	1 strand	Very deep dusky pink (DMC)
56	2mm	Light mustard green
44	2mm	Medium sky blue
15	2mm	Bright yellow
31	2mm	Light apple green

Colours for each individual flower and corresponding leaf colour have been grouped together to allow you to work each group as it is illustrated.

Requirements

Fabric, 10cm x 10cm. (This will be sufficient fabric for 1 brooch and will fit into a 7.5cm hoop).

Turned timber brooch blank (See Stockists).

Metal brooch clip, glue-on type.

Sewing cotton to match fabric colour.

PVA glue.

Ribbons and threads as listed to complete chosen design.

Scrap of thin cardboard — similar thickness to a business card.

Scrap of thin wadding for padding the brooch.

Method

1 Cut a circle from the thin cardboard to fit neatly into the timber brooch blank.

2 Using a water erasable pen trace around the brooch blank onto the centre of the fabric.

3 Using doubled sewing thread, work a fine row of running stitches 6 - 8 mm outside the blue line. These stitches are used to draw the fabric around the wooden blank after the embroidery is complete. By doubling the threads you give them additional strength so they can be pulled tightly.

4 Fit the fabric into the hoop and ensure that it is drum tight.

5 Embroider the chosen design inside the blue line. See instructions and illustrations for individual designs and for the complete list of ribbon and thread colours used.

6 Remove fabric from hoop and apply cold water to blue line to erase this completely.

7 Cut out circle of embroidery carefully approximately 6 - 8mm outside the row of gathering stitches.

8 Cut a circle of wadding the same size as the circle of cardboard.

9 Place the wadding and the cardboard face down on the back of the embroidery, ensuring that the circles are centred on your work and gently pull both ends of the running stitches to draw the fabric around the cardboard. It should be a firm fit. Adjust the gathers so that they are even and invisible from the front of the brooch. Tie off the ends of the gathering threads.

10 Using PVA or craft glue spread a small, even amount inside the timber recess of the brooch blank, carefully placing your embroidery inside this recess. Hold firmly until the glue adheres.

11 Glue the metal brooch clip into place, centred from right to left and slightly above the middle of the timber brooch blank.

Hair Barrettes

Two individual designs have been included, although the rose design has an alternative colour grouping of ribbons and threads as listed below. The two rose design layouts are slightly different just to give you an idea of how easily designs may be changed to compliment different projects and applications.

Rose Spray (Blue)

44	4mm	Medium sky blue
90	4mm	Very pale sky blue
33	2mm	Medium blue green
926	1 strand	Rajmahal
13	2mm	Pale lemon
15	2mm	Bright yellow

Madeira metallic thread — silver

Rose Spray (Pink)

159	4mm	Dark dusky pink
158	4mm	Medium dusky pink
20	2mm	Medium grass green
521	1 strand	Rajmahal
5	2mm	Very pale pink
15	2mm	Bright yellow

Madeira metallic thread — gold No 6.

The metallic threads are used at the completion of the ribbon embroidery to add highlights in the spaces between the flower sprays. These highlights are worked in a fine feather stitch to form the fine branch-like effect.

Carpet of Flowers

Ribbons and threads used are as for those listed for the Carpet of Flowers brooch. The thread and ribbon reference numbers, along with the colour description, will allow you to work each colour combination as they are listed. Refer to the diagram and the photograph to help you position each individual flower and foliage grouping.

REQUIREMENTS

Fabric, 20cm x 20cm. (This will be sufficient fabric for one hair barrette and will fit into a 12.5cm [5 - 6"] hoop.)

Commercially-available fabric-covered hair barrette.

Sewing cotton to match fabric colour.

Ribbons and threads to complete design chosen.

Method

1 Remove existing fabric from hair barrette by gently easing the metal edges apart with a thin flat object.

2 Trace the shape of the barrette onto the fabric with water erasable pen. This forms the outer boundary of the embroidery.

3 Work a row of fine running stitches, 1cm outside the blue line using a doubled length of sewing thread. Leave both ends of this thread approximately 5cm long.

4 Work your chosen embroidery design inside the blue line referring to the illustration and the photograph for placement and colours used.

5 Remove fabric from hoop and, using cold water, erase the blue line.

6 Cut out the shape of the barrette carefully, approximately 6 - 8mm outside the row of gathering stitches.

7 Place the barrette slide face down onto the back of the embroidery and carefully pull the ends of the running stitches until they are tight. Even out the gathers around the perimeter of the barrette. Tie the ends firmly.

8 Fit the back of the barrette into position and squeeze the edges of the metal form towards the backing frame until both pieces fit snugly together once again.

Silk Keepsake Bag with Pansies

This tiny bag was inspired by the colour of the silk which forms the lining and the internal pockets. I saw the fabric and thought how lovely it would look with the rich colours one normally associates with pansies, a favourite flower of mine.

A simple garland of pansies decorates the outside of the bag.

Ribbons and threads required

178	7mm	Light grape
15	7mm	Bright yellow
85	7mm	Deep purple
4	4mm	Black
15	4mm	Bright yellow
13	4mm	Pale lemon
20	7mm	Medium grass green
521	1 strand	Rajmahal
Ecru	1 strand	Rajmahal

Madeira metallic thread — gold No 6 (This is only required if you wish to include a tiny spider web amongst the pansies as I have done.)

Centres for the mauve and purple pansies are worked in bright yellow French knots. Centres for the yellow pansies are worked in pale lemon French knots. All the full pansy flowers have black silk ribbon details and straight stitch detail worked in 1 strand of Rajmahal silk thread, Ecru. For further details on working the pansies please refer to them in the chapter detailing the formation and stitches used to form the flowers.

Requirements

Fabric, 40cm black Dupion silk, 40cm deep purple Dupion silk.

1.5 metres of thin black cord.

Matching sewing threads, deep purple and black.

Silk ribbons and threads as per design requirements above.

Scrap of thick cardboard and quilters wadding for internal base.

2 decorative beads for cord ends.

Method

1 Mark and cut out 1 x 40cm circle from each piece of fabric. The black is for the outside of the bag, the purple is the lining.

2 Overlock or zig zag around the edges of the silk circles to prevent them fraying.

3 Mark in the centre of the black fabric a 20cm circle. This line forms the guide line for the garland of pansies. A white pencil can be used to mark this but use it very lightly.

4 Fit the fabric into a large hoop. 30cm is ideal.

5 Embroider the pansies around the guide line referring to the diagram for positioning details.

6 Work two small buttonholes, on the black circle only, inside the lines of stitching which will form the casing for the cord. Care needs to be taken here to place these buttonholes accurately. Don't forget to take into account seam allowances etc. when positioning them prior to sewing (See Step 14).

7 Cut out and sew together 2 circles of deep purple silk, 26cm in diameter, leaving a 3cm opening. Turn the circles through to the right side and slip stitch opening closed. (You may like to bind the edges of these 2 circles together with a bias tape made from the black silk as an alternative method of joining them together.)

8 Centre this smaller circle onto the deep purple of lining fabric.

9 Sew this smaller circle onto the lining by stitching across the centre of the inner circle from one edge to the other 4 times as illustrated. These four rows of stitching segment the inner circle into 8 equal portions.

10 Place the right sides of the lining section and the embroidered section together, sew around the outside of the circle leaving a 3cm gap for turning. Turn to the right side and slip stitch opening closed.

11 Cut one 11cm circle from thick cardboard and the scrap of thin wadding, cover this with a circle of black silk.

12 Centre this fabric-covered cardboard base into the bottom of the bag and slip stitch into place through the lining fabric only.

13 The segments that are created in the smaller internal circle become the storage pockets for the jewellery when the bag is closed.

14 Sew two rows of machine stitching around the outside edge of the bag, the first 2.5cm in from the edge and the second 4cm in from the outside edge. The buttonholes worked in Step 6 must fall in between these lines of machine stitching.

15 Cut open the buttonholes, ensuring you only cut the black fabric.

16 Cut the length of cord in half and thread one piece through a buttonhole, around the entire bag and out the same buttonhole. Thread the other piece of cord through the other buttonhole in the same manner. By pulling both cords together at the same time the bag will close evenly.

17 Tie the ends of the cords together and decorate each with a bead if desired.

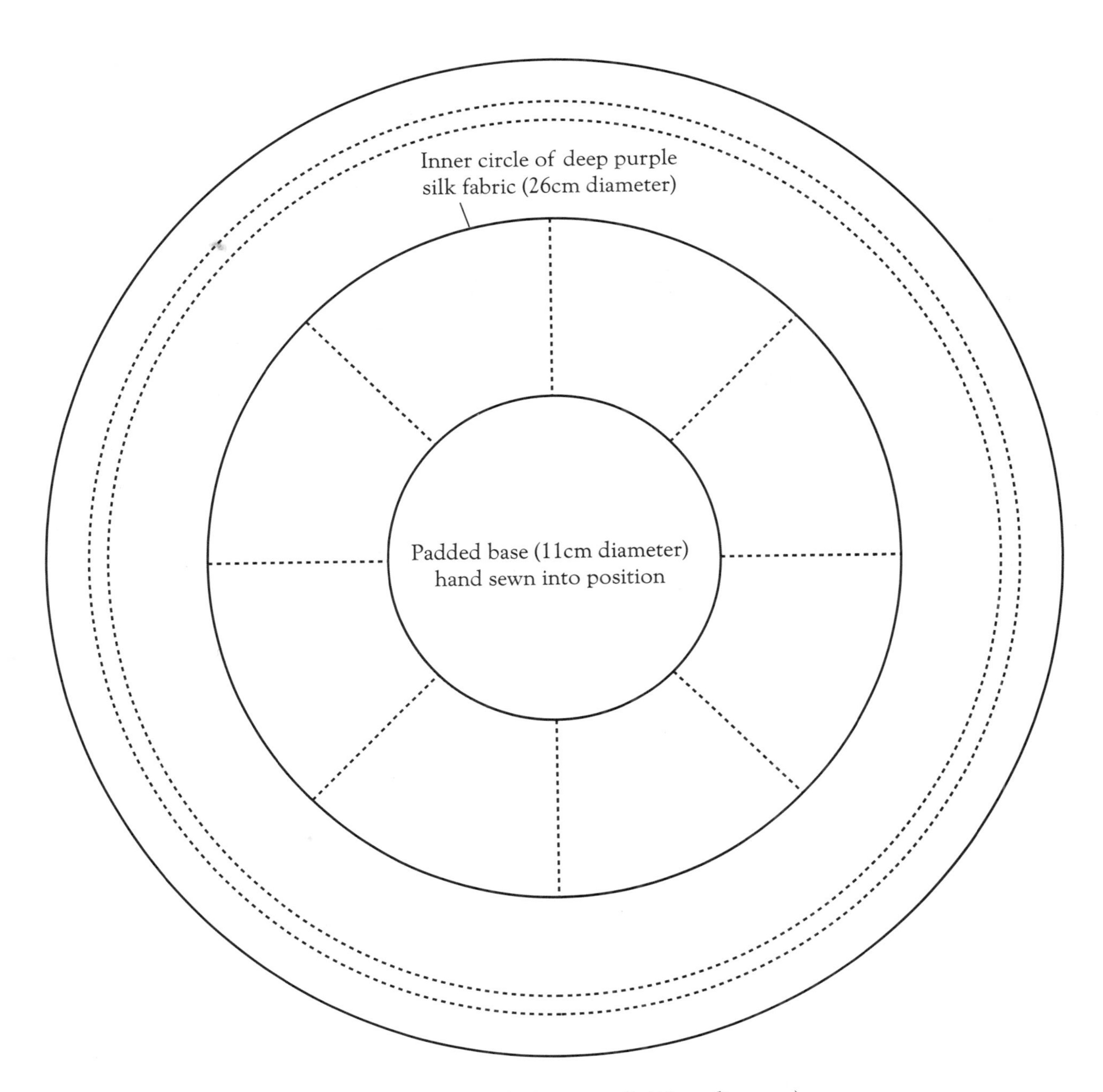

Circle of deep purple Dupion silk (40cm diameter)

---------- rows of machine stitching

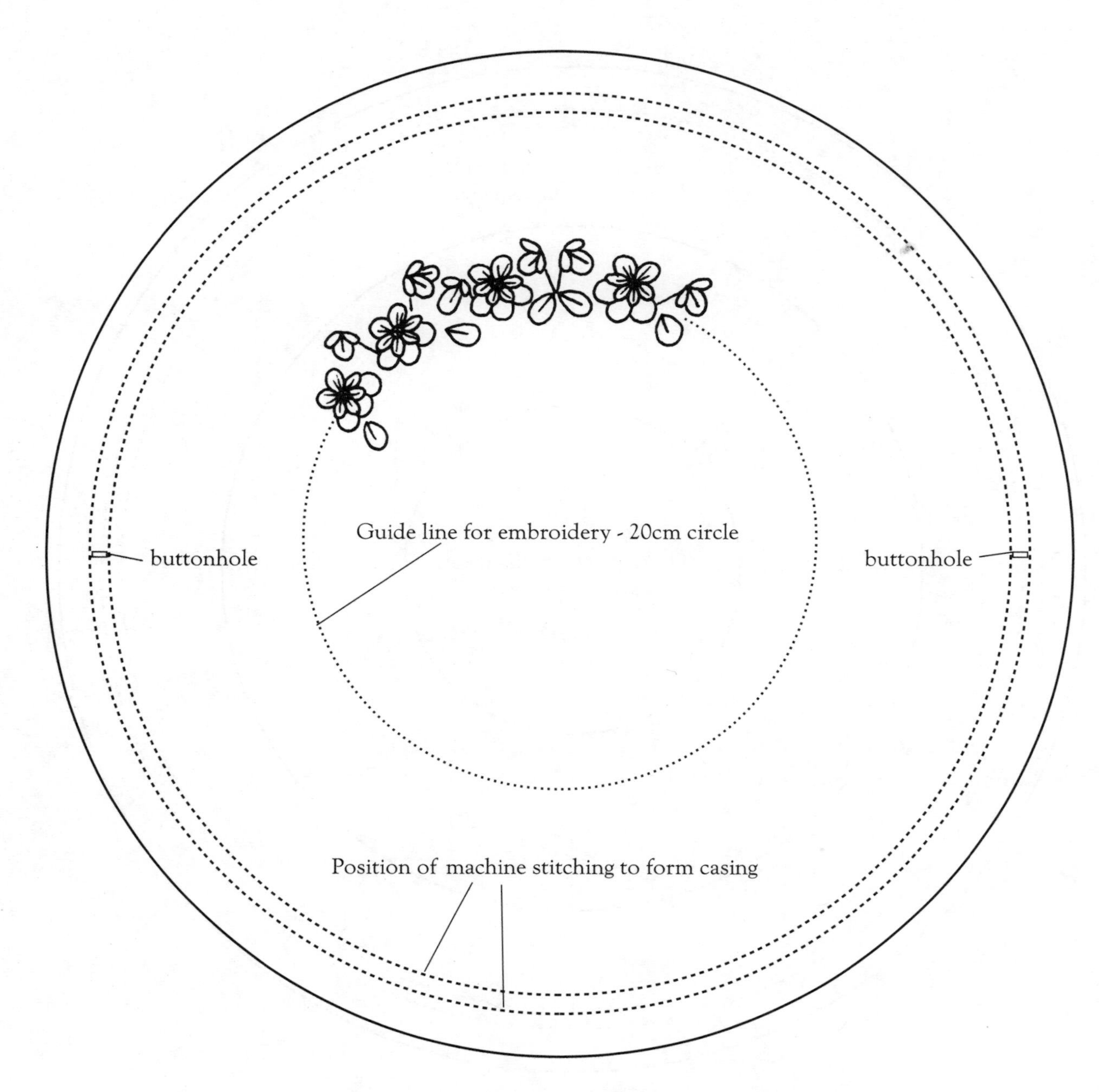

Circle of black Dupion silk (40cm diameter)

Sewer's Holdall Bag with Flower Samplers

This handy drawstring bag was designed to be roomy enough to hold your sewing requirements, easy to close and very portable.

The exterior of the bag is divided into eight segments and each is embroidered with a different group of flowers.

It is an ideal project to teach yourself the basic stitches and construction of flower groups as well as being something I have found very useful.

Requirements

70cm of cotton fabric. The one I have used has a tiny overall design on it which does not overpower the embroidery but helps to add interest.

70cm of cotton fabric for the lining. You can use a plain fabric for this but I always like to use a beautiful print for the lining. When you open the bag it is always a pleasant surprise.

3 metres of twisted cording.

Sewing threads, pins, scissors etc.

4 decorative beads to finish the cord ends.

Ribbons and threads to complete each embroidery (These are listed in flower groupings as they are worked around the bag.)

Thick cardboard and a scrap of quilters wadding.

The following drawings of all the flower groups are the actual size as they appear on the bag.

A complete list of threads and ribbons and their widths, along with the colour description as used for each individual floral group, as well as some helpful sewing notes have been included below. But please refer to the chapter containing the flower drawings and instructions if you are unsure of the order of work.

1 Arum lilies and Grape Hyacinths

Flower	3	7mm	White
Leaf	20	7mm	Medium grass green
Stem	3346	1 strand	Medium grass green ,DMC
Detail	444	3 strands	Bright yellow, DMC
Leaf	170	4mm	Light yellow green
Stem	734	1 strand	Light yellow green
Flower	118	4mm	Deep blue mauve

2 Daisies

Note: For clarity on the illustration, stitches forming only the daisies and buds have been detailed as ribbon stitch; but the leaves are also formed using basic ribbon stitch.

Leaf	31	2mm	Light apple green
Stem	523	1 strand	Light apple green, DMC
Centre	15	4mm	Bright yellow
Petals	128	2mm	Raspberry pink

3 Iris

Extended and couched ribbon stitch has been used to form the leaves and this has a fine running stitch formed down the centre of each leaf. To add further interest, iris flowers and buds have been formed in three shades of mauve.

Leaf	32	4mm	Light blue green
Stem	3817	1 strand	Light blue green, DMC
Flowers	118	4mm	Deep blue mauve
	22	4mm	Light mauve
	178	4mm	Light grape

4 Rose bush

Full roses have a French knot centre formed in light copper brown.

Once again, for clarity, and to help distinguish between buds and leaves on the illustration, only the buds have been shown as ribbon stitch but all the leaves are also formed using basic ribbon stitch.

Leaf	21	4mm	Dark forest green
Stem	319	1 strand	Dark forest green, DMC
Centre	36	4mm	Light copper brown
Flower	13	4mm	Pale lemon
Web	Madeira metallic thread - silver		
Spider	310	1 strand	Black, DMC

5 Violets

To add interest, violet flowers and buds have been formed using three colours. The centres of all the flowers are formed using bright yellow.

Leaf	20	7mm	Medium grass green
Stem	3346	1 strand	Medium grass green, DMC
Flowers	84	4mm	Purple
	22	4mm	Light mauve
	163	4mm	Very light rose pink
	15	4mm	Bright yellow

6 Foxgloves

Three shades of blue have been used to form the flower stalks. The darker of these is used to form the 'front' flower and the lighter shades are used to form the flower stalks which appear behind. The individual stitches used to form the stalks are made using basic ribbon stitch.

Leaf	62	4mm	Light ice green
Stem	369	1 strand	Light ice green, DMC
Flowers	90	4mm	Very pale sky blue
	44	4mm	Medium sky blue
	45	4mm	Deep blue

7 Daisies

The leaves of this bush have also been formed using extended and couched ribbon stitch. The fine running stitch detail has been added after the leaves have been formed.

Leaf	20	4mm	Medium grass green
Stem	3346	1 strand	Medium grass green, DMC
Flower	1	4mm	Antique white
Centre	15	4mm	Bright yellow

8 Briar Rose

Flower centres are a French knot worked in pale lemon ribbon; the pistil stitch details are added with matching DMC thread.

Leaf	62	4mm	Light ice green
Stem	369	1 strand	Light ice green, DMC
Flowers	158	7mm	Medium dusky pink
Buds	159	7mm	Deep dusky pink
Centre	13	4mm	Pale lemon
Detail	745	1 strand	Pale lemon

Method

1 Mark and cut out the circles of fabric for the exterior of the bag and the lining. They include a seam allowance of 5mm.

2 On the circle of fabric to be used for the bag, use your blue water erasable pen to mark 8 equal segments.

3 Draw a circle on the fabric to mark the position of the base of the flowers. This circle is 32cm in diameter.

4 Embroider each flower group in the individual segments. You will be able to use a 20cm (8") hoop to hold the fabric taught as you embroider. Take care not to squash any completed embroidery in the hoop as you move to the next segment.

5 Work a row of feather stitch on the segment

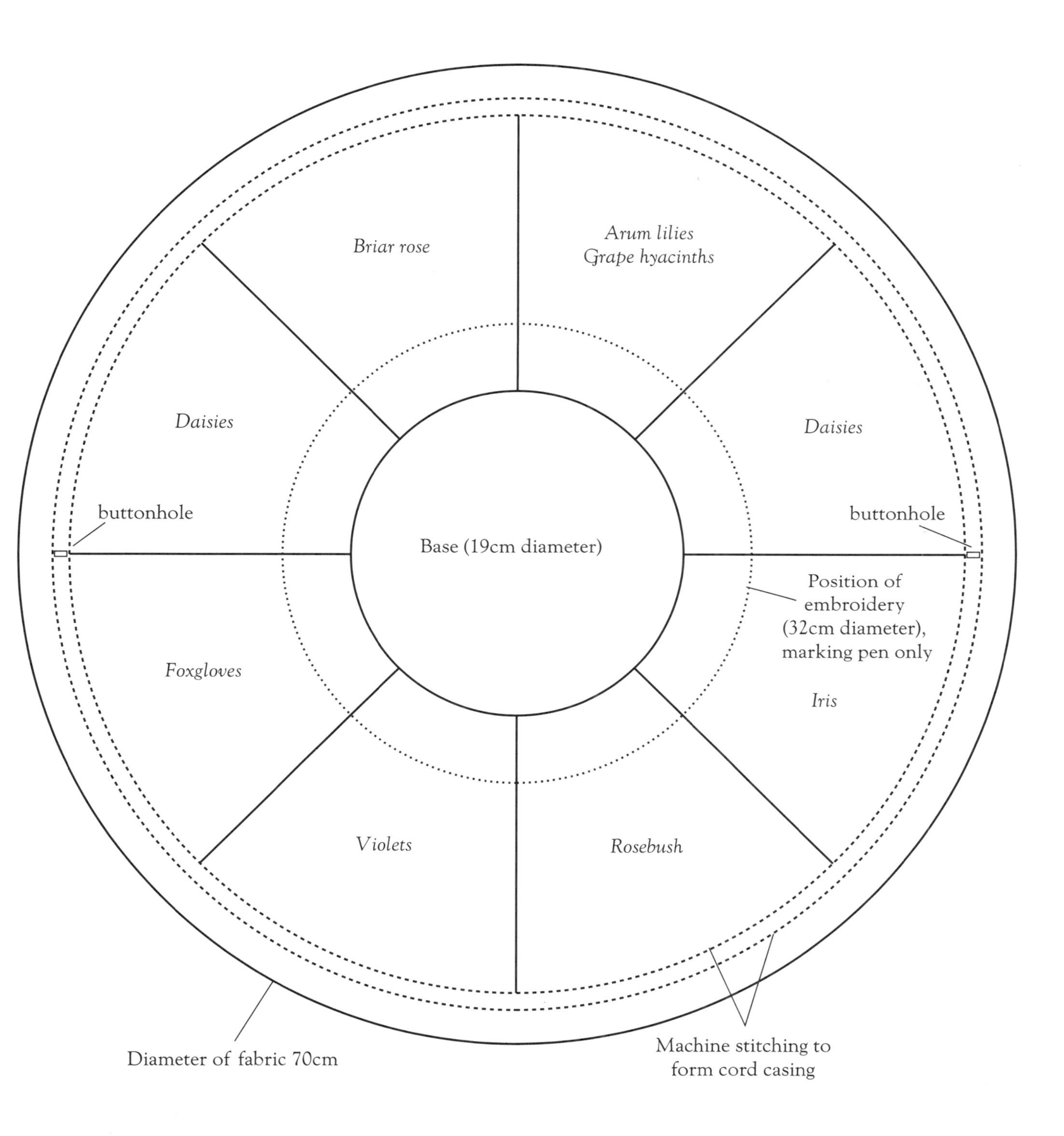
Briar rose
Arum lilies
Grape hyacinths
Daisies
Daisies
buttonhole
buttonhole
Base (19cm diameter)
Position of embroidery (32cm diameter), marking pen only
Foxgloves
Iris
Violets
Rosebush
Diameter of fabric 70cm
Machine stitching to form cord casing

dividing lines as on the sample project if you wish to permanently divide the flowers into their individual positions. This row of stitching is 17cm long.

6 Use cold water to remove any visible blue lines at this time.

7 Work two, 1cm buttonholes on opposite sides of the circle, 2.5cm in from the outer edge. Take care when positioning these buttonholes as they must fall between the lines of machine stitching which will create the casing band when the bag is assembled.

8 With wrong sides together sew the lining to the outside of the bag, 5mm in from the edge, leaving a gap of 5cm to allow for turning.

9 Turn circles to the right side and slip stitch opening closed.

10 Press the edges carefully, avoiding the embroidery.

11 Mark and sew the two lines of machine stitching which form the cord casing.

12 Carefully cut the buttonholes open and thread the cord, cut into two equal lengths through the buttonholes. Each piece of cord is threaded through one buttonhole, around the entire bag and out through the same buttonhole. Add the decorative beads to the cords after the ends are tied together.

13 Cut a 19cm circle from a piece of thick cardboard, cover this with a scrap of wadding. Cut a circle of fabric from the same material as the exterior of the bag and cover the cardboard circle. This will form a firm base for the bag.

14 Centre this base onto the exterior of the bag and slip stitch neatly into place.

Your bag is now complete, I hope you enjoy using it.

The Painted Backgrounds

The painted backgrounds pictured in the landscapes in this book have become a feature of my work and have given me the opportunity to create more natural-looking garden landscapes. By applying paint to the fabric before commencing an embroidery I am able to build up different tones on the fabric and these form the background to the silk ribbon embroidery. The colours used to create the garden features and the background to the flowers add additional dimension and a real sense of perspective to the completed embroidery.

I use folk art paint or dry brush acrylic paint, the type used for fabric painting, to colour the fabric prior to the embroidery. The fabric is what is commonly known as seeded homespun. There are different qualities available so make sure you choose a good quality one. A complete list of the paint colours used follows the directions below.

You may like to experiment with some paints you have at home. Check to see if they are colourfast first by applying them to fabric, allowing them to dry completely and then washing in warm water. If your sample piece does not run or bleed then you can assume that the paint is suitable to create a background for embroidery. Although it is unlikely you will wash your completed landscape embroideries, because, like me, you will probably frame them behind glass, you will have to remove fabric marker pen lines.

You need not be an accomplished artist to be able to apply paint to create a suitable embroidery background. If you are confident with the painting techniques you may like to use more colour but do keep in mind that the silk ribbon embroidery will be the feature of the work and the background is there simply to enhance this.

Some of the painted backgrounds are more complicated than others, but the techniques used to create these remain the same.

A small amount of paint is squeezed onto a tile or plate and water is also put on the plate. Using a soft bristle brush, a little of the paint is drawn across and mixed with the water to create a water colour consistency 'wash'. This wash of colour is dabbed onto the fabric where that colour is required. The deeper shades of a colour are built up simply by adding further paint until the desired depth of colour is achieved.

It is impossible to remove excess colour once it is applied, so it is important that the areas of colour are well-defined before beginning the paint applications and that areas of deep colour are built up slowly.

There is no need to wait for an area to dry before applying more of the same colour but it is important that an area does not become saturated with water as this may cause paint to bleed to an adjacent area. If the fabric does become too 'wet' simply dry it with a hair dryer before continuing. Always ensure that one area of colour is completely dry before attempting to add different colours in adjoining areas. Always wash your brush in clean water before attempting to apply another colour.

On the painted backgrounds featured here I have used a maximum of 3 - 4 colours. The paints I have used on these backgrounds are as follows —

Folk Art Acrylic Colour by PLAID. (These paints are commonly available in craft shops, folk art suppliers and larger fabric chain stores.) The colour description given with each of the paints will give you an indication of shade should you wish to substitute another paint brand.

902	Taffy	a deep cream
942	Honeycomb	a light tan
923	Clover	a medium olive green
924	Thicket	a dark olive green
910	Slate blue	a deep blue grey

If you are unsure whether you will be able to control the paint to fill in some of the finer detail areas, such as the mortar lines in '*The Old Stone Wall*' or the rose support in '*Jessie's Garden*', then these details can be added with a suitable coloured pencil when the fabric has been painted and is completely dry. A 'Pygma' pen may also be used. Similarly a coloured pencil, or a 'Pygma' pen may be useful to add or enhance additional details if you need at the completion of the embroidery.

The Garden Landscapes

Following are the details and illustrations to complete each of the four garden landscapes featured in this book.

I have given, for each landscape, a complete list of all the silk ribbons used, their widths and their colours if you wish to substitute. Rajmahal stranded silk thread has been used exclusively for the detail stitching on each of the works. A single thread has been used unless otherwise noted. I have also included for your reference the thread number for DMC stranded cotton should you wish to substitute this thread.

For each garden landscape there are two detailed drawings.

1. Design Template

The first drawing is the design template which will give you the size of the work as well as the position of the garden 'feature'. This drawing also has an additional dotted line detail which represents the change of colour line for the pathway as featured in three of the landscapes.

The feature of the garden should be marked very lightly with a sharp HB pencil. The outside boundary edge of the embroidery, as well as the position of the path, needs to be marked with a water erasable pen. Stem stitch, or alternatively a 'Pygma' pen line, will cover the fine pencil lines after painting is completed. The marker line indicating the path position can be removed after painting, but usually it will disappear as you paint the area with the colours used to create the path.

You may find it useful before starting to paint the green flower background to position the second detailed drawing, the flower positioning diagram, beneath your fabric to ascertain areas where the green paint wash needs to be applied. The green is concentrated more heavily in the foreground and fades out to a very light wash as you work towards the edge of the flower embroidery.

Always ensure that an area is completely dry before changing colours to paint an adjacent area. The painted background must be completely dry before adding details with a 'Pygma' pen.

2 Flower Position Diagram

The flower position diagram has been prepared to indicate the amount of area that each particular flower group uses. The lines do not indicate the number of leaves on a particular plant but just the space the completed plant will use. Please refer to the individual flower guides for the stitching details for each plant group.

Following are some guidelines which I keep in mind when creating a garden landscape. You may find them useful to create one of your own.

1 Generally flowers or bushes which appear in the background are worked first. If you work from the top of the work down this will allow you to overlap flowers if appropriate to create additional depth.

2 Background flowers are worked in more subdued and softer shades. Foreground flowers can incorporate richer, darker colours. The darker colours used in the foreground tend to make the flower appear to be in front of others and thus help to create depth in your work.

3 Impressions of flowers in the background are created using a minimum of stitches. Most are created with a simple stem stitch and leaves are formed with a basic ribbon stitch and flowers formed with a French knot. With the lack of visible detail this also adds to the impression of depth.

4 Flowers which are normally quite small and insignificant in size in an overall garden scheme, such as violets, forget me knots, pansies, etc. are worked in the foreground to once again increase the sense of depth.

5 Added thread details, such as the vein in a violet or pansy leaf, or the straight stitching on a pansy flower, as well as the choice of wider ribbons for the leaves of these flowers, also create depth within the work. Fine, detailed stitching is only added in the foreground flowers.

The Rose

This is the smallest and simplest of the garden landscapes and includes a deep red standard rose as the central feature and a portion of an old post and rail fence. A simple garden path meanders through the flowers.

Rajmahal stranded silk thread has been used to add the details and the stems in the work, but I have also included the DMC alternative thread should you wish to substitute this.

Applying the Paint

a Using the feature diagram underneath your fabric, mark the outer edge of the work and the position of the path with a water erasable pen. Using a brown 'Pygma' pen lightly mark in the outline of the post and rail fence.

b Using the paints 902, 942, a light touch and horizontal brush strokes, paint in the path. Using the same colours carefully fill in the post and rail fence. Allow these areas to dry completely.

c Refer to the flower positioning diagram and carefully gauge the areas of the fabric which need to be painted with a green wash of colour, 923, 924. The wash of colour is confined to areas which are to be embroidered. The deeper shades are kept in the foreground areas and the painted areas are lighter in the background of the landscape. The chapter on the painted backgrounds details how to create a light 'wash' of colour.

d Refer to the flower positioning diagram to mark the placement of stems, etc, using a water erasable pen.

e The guide following indicates the threads and ribbons used for each flower grouping.

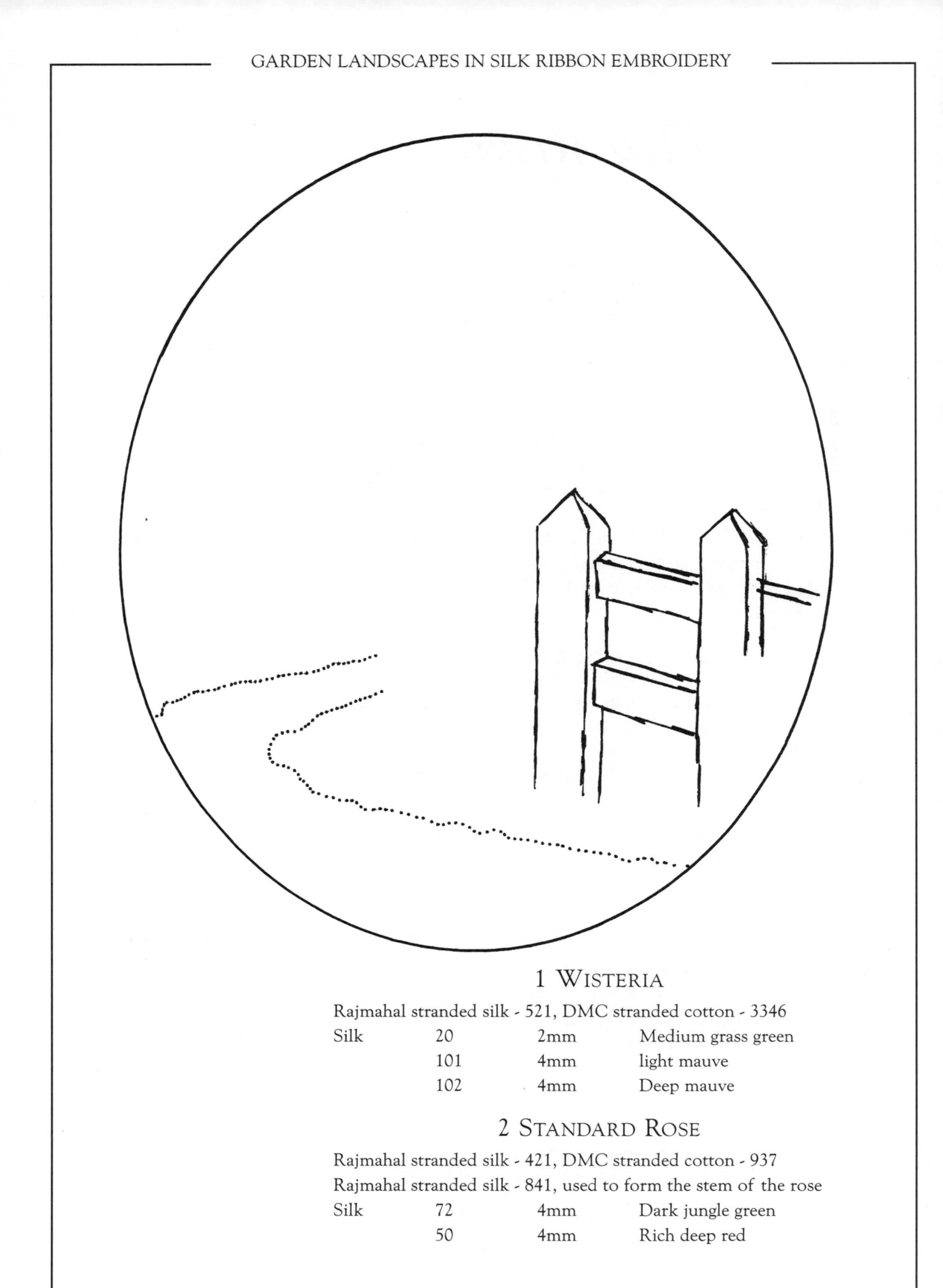

1 Wisteria

Rajmahal stranded silk - 521, DMC stranded cotton - 3346

Silk	20	2mm	Medium grass green
	101	4mm	light mauve
	102	4mm	Deep mauve

2 Standard Rose

Rajmahal stranded silk - 421, DMC stranded cotton - 937

Rajmahal stranded silk - 841, used to form the stem of the rose

Silk	72	4mm	Dark jungle green
	50	4mm	Rich deep red

3 Lavender

Rajmahal stranded silk - 926, DMC stranded cotton - 520

Silk	33	2mm	Medium blue green
	101	4mm	Light mauve
	178	4mm	Light grape

4 Forget me Knots

Silk	31	2mm	Light apple green
	44	4mm	Medium sky blue
	15	4mm	Bright yellow

5 VIOLETS

Rajmahal stranded silk - 521, DMC stranded cotton - 3346

Silk	20	4mm	Medium grass green
	85	4mm	Deep purple
	15	4mm	Bright yellow

6 PINK DAISIES

Silk	33	4mm	Medium blue green
	112	4mm	Light rose pink
	15	4mm	Bright yellow

7 YELLOW DAISIES

Silk	21	2mm	Dark forest green
	15	2mm	Bright yellow
	1	4mm	Antique white

8 IRIS

Rajmahal stranded silk - 926, DMC stranded cotton - 3817
Rajmahal stranded silk - Ecru, straight stitch detail to flowers

Silk	33	4mm	Medium blue green
	55	4mm	Dark gold
	13	2mm	Pale lemon

9 LILY OF THE VALLEY

Rajmahal stranded silk - 521, DMC stranded cotton - 470

Silk	171	4mm	Medium olive green
	3	4mm	White

Jessie's Garden

This garden landscape features a weeping standard rose which grows in our garden. This rose overlooks a place in the garden where a much loved family pet was buried after being hit by a car, hence the name. It remains one of my favourite embroideries.

This is an enjoyable garden landscape to work as the feature is simply the rose support. The background is painted before positioning the flowers to increase the amount of depth created by each of the flower groups in the garden landscape.

The silk ribbons that I have used are listed below as well as the reference numbers for the Rajmahal stranded silk thread. DMC stranded cotton reference numbers have also been included should you wish to substitute.

The flower groups are listed to correspond to the number appearing on the the positioning diagram

Applying the paint

a Using the feature diagram underneath your fabric, mark the outer edge of the work. Using a sharp pencil, lightly mark in the position of the rose support.

b Using the paint 910, and a thin brush, carefully paint in the rose support. The centre pole of the rose support is stitched in stem stitch during the embroidery so the edges will be detailed sharply at this stage. Allow this paint to dry completely before commencing another colour.

c Refer to the flower positioning diagram and carefully gauge the areas of fabric inside the border which need to be coloured with a light green paint wash, 923, 924. The wash needs to be applied only to areas

enlarge to 133%

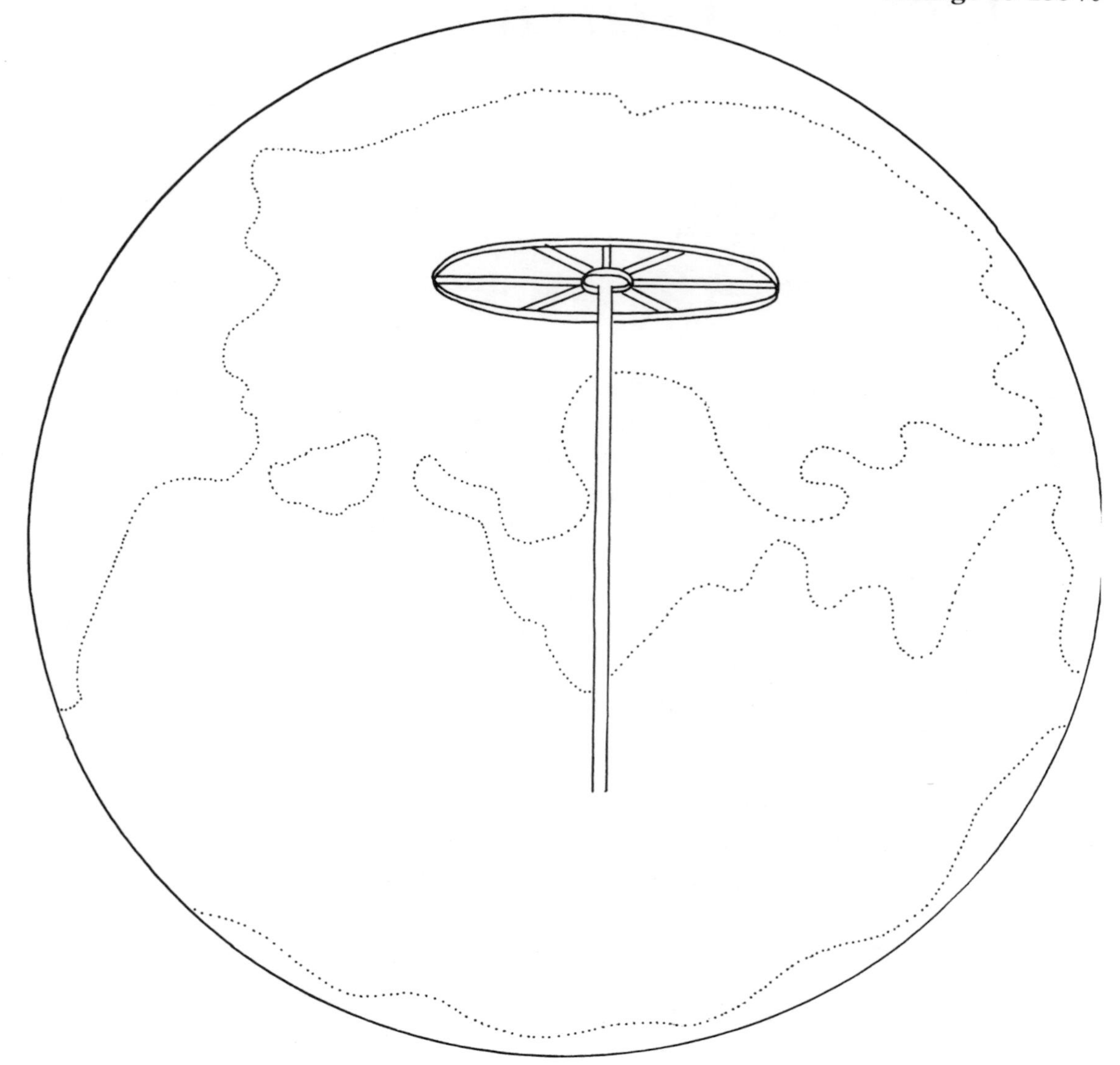

which will be covered by embroidery. The chapter on the painted backgrounds details how to create a light 'wash' of colour. Once again the darker wash is used in the foreground with the colour fading as you near the edge of the embroidery.

d Refer to the flower positioning diagram to mark the placement of stems, etc, using a water erasable pen.

e The guide below indicates the threads and ribbons used for each flower grouping.

enlarge to 133%

1 Weeping Standard Rose

Rose support - Rajmahal stranded silk - 226, DMC - 318
Stem of Rose - Rajmahal stranded silk - 841, DMC - 841
Rajmahal stranded silk - 65, DMC stranded cotton - 319

Silk	21	4mm	Dark forest green
	157	4mm	Very light dusky pink
Spark Organdy	32	9mm	Green - for additional optional leaves

2 Iris

Rajmahal stranded silk - 805, DMC stranded cotton - 3817
Rajmahal stranded silk - Ecru, straight stitch detail to flowers

Silk	33	4mm	Medium blue green
	13	4mm	Pale lemon

3 Blue flowering foliage

Rajmahal stranded silk - 421, DMC stranded cotton - 369

Silk	31	2mm	Light apple green
	125	4mm	Light blue

4 Gerbera

Rajmahal stranded silk - 65, DMC stranded cotton - 319

Silk	21	2mm	Dark forest green
	128	2mm	Raspberry pink
	13	4mm	Pale lemon

5 Grape Hyacinths

Rajmahal stranded silk - 421, DMC stranded cotton - 470

Silk	171	4mm	Medium olive green
	102	4mm	Deep violet

6 Lily of the Valley

Rajmahal stranded silk - 421, DMC stranded cotton - 937

Silk	72	4mm	Dark jungle green
	3	4mm	White

7 Pink Daisies

Silk	163	4mm	Very light rose pink
	15	4mm	Bright yellow

8 Forget Me Knots

Silk	33	2mm	Medium blue green
	125	4mm	Light blue
	15	4mm	Bright yellow

9 Bluebells

Rajmahal stranded silk - 65, DMC stranded cotton - 319

Silk	21	2mm	Dark forest green
	126	2mm	Medium blue grey

10 Violets

Rajmahal stranded silk - 51, DMC stranded cotton - 3346

Silk	20	4mm	Medium grass green
	84	4mm	Purple
	15	4mm	Bright yellow

11 Mauve Daisies

Rajmahal stranded silk - 521, DMC stranded cotton - 3346

Silk	20	4mm	Medium grass green
	178	4mm	Light grape
	15	4mm	Bright yellow

12 Snowdrops

Rajmahal stranded silk - 926, DMC stranded cotton - 3817

Silk	33	2mm	Medium blue green
	13	2mm	Pale lemon

13 Pale Pink Daisies

Silk	157	4mm	Very light dusky pink
	128	4mm	Raspberry pink
	72	4mm	Dark jungle green

14 Burgundy Flowering Foliage

Rajmahal stranded silk - 802, DMC stranded cotton - 369

Silk	31	4mm	Light apple green
	130	4mm	Deep burgundy

The Old Stone Wall

Another favourite idea of mine is a garden divided into 'rooms' by means of walls, arches or other features, hence the inspiration for the stone wall. This divides the garden from other areas which we are able to glimpse through the opening. The gravel path adds to the sense of perspective and leads our eye to the garden beyond the wall.

Once again Rajmahal stranded silk thread has been used exclusively with the silk ribbons to create the flowers. If you wish to substitute DMC stranded cotton the reference number has been included.

Applying the paint

a Using the feature diagram underneath your fabric, mark the outer edge of the work and the position of the path with a water erasable pen.

b With a pencil very lightly mark in the blocks which create the old stone wall. (Only the paint will be used to create this wall so keep the pencil marks as light as possible.)

c Using the paints 902, 942, a light touch and horizontal brush strokes, paint in the path. Dry this area completely before using the same colours to fill in the blocks of the stone wall.

d Using the slate grey colour, 901, and a fine brush, add the delicate mortar lines between the blocks. Dry this completely.

e Refer to the flower positioning diagram and carefully gauge the areas which need to be coloured with

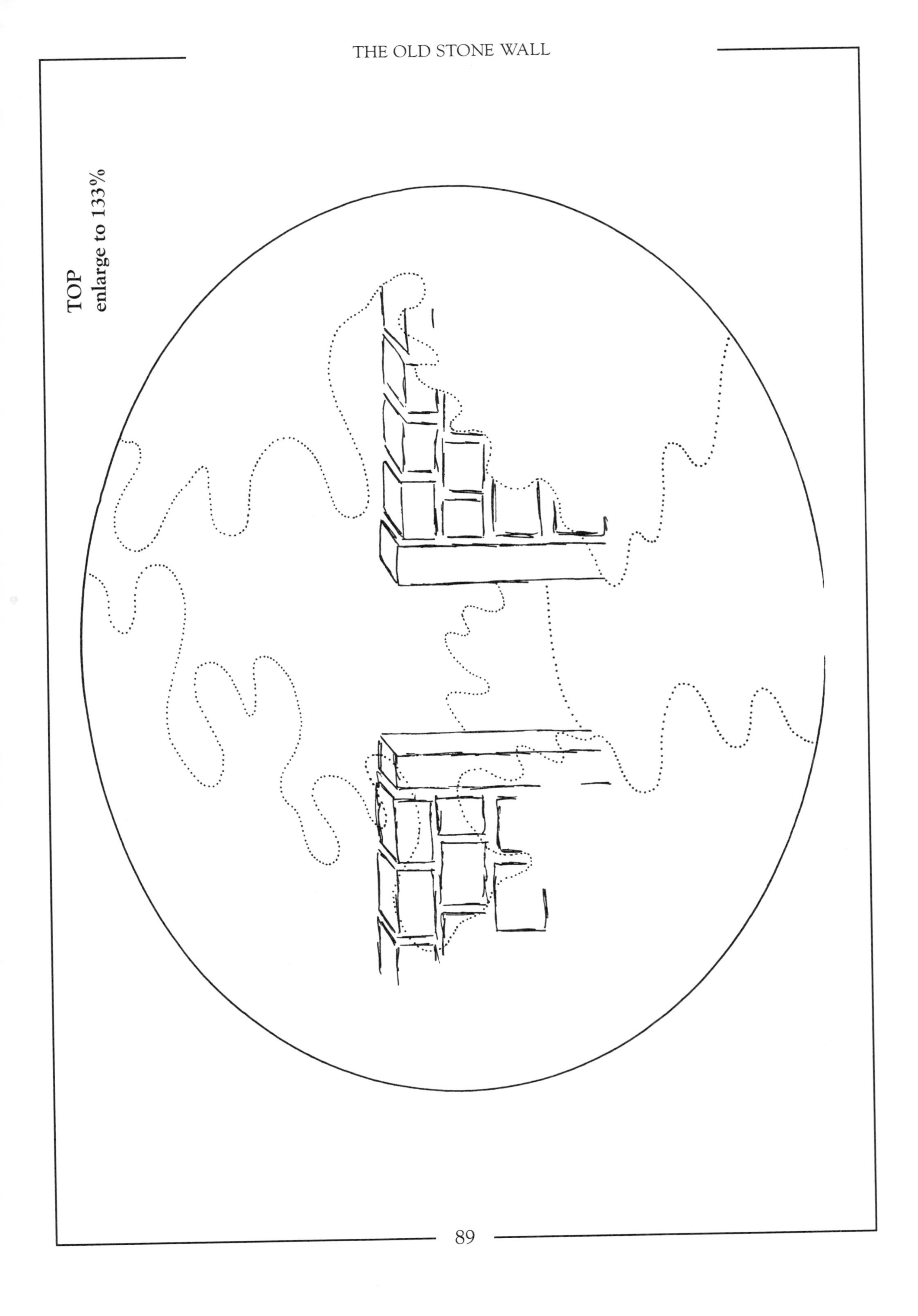
TOP
enlarge to 133%

TOP
enlarge to 133%
1
2
3
4
5
6
7
8
9
10
11
12
13
14
15
16
17
18
19
20
21
22
23

a green 'wash' of paint, 923, 924. The 'wash' of colour is only applied where the embroidery will be worked. Once again the deeper shades of green are contained in the foreground and the wash becomes lighter and more subtle in the background areas.

f Refer to the flower positioning diagram to mark the placement of stems, etc, using a water erasable pen.

g Flowers, and the threads and ribbons used to create them have been listed on the following pages in three groupings: those on the left of the work, those on the right side of the work and the background flowers seen through the opening.

Left Hand Side

1 Pink Flowering Foliage

Rajmahal stranded silk - 841, 2 strands, DMC - 841, 2 strands

Silk	20	4mm	Medium grass green
	127	4mm	Light raspberry pink
Spark organdy	32	9mm	Green - for additional optional leaves

2 Iris

Rajmahal stranded silk - 805, DMC stranded cotton - 520
Rajmahal stranded silk - 261 - Lemon, to detail straight stitching on flowers

Silk	33	4mm	Medium blue green
	1	4mm	Antique white

3 Pink Daisy

Silk	20	4mm	Medium grass green
	163	4mm	Very light rose pink
	15	4mm	Bright yellow

4 Lavender

Rajmahal stranded silk - 926, DMC stranded cotton - 3817

Silk	32	2mm	Light blue green
	22	4mm	Light mauve

5 Yellow Flowering Foliage

Rajmahal stranded silk - 65, DMC stranded cotton - 319

Silk	21	4mm	Medium grass green
	15	4mm	Bright yellow

6 Lemon Daisies

Silk	14	4mm	Deep lemon
	15	4mm	Bright yellow
	72	4mm	Dark jungle green

7 Bluebells

Rajmahal stranded silk - 65, DMC stranded cotton - 319

Silk	21	2mm	Dark forest green
	126	2mm	Medium blue grey

8 Violets

Rajmahal stranded silk - 521, DMC stranded cotton - 3346

Silk	20	7mm	Medium grass green
	84	4mm	Purple
	15	4mm	Bright yellow

9 Forget Me Knots

Silk	8	4mm	Pale pink
	15	4mm	Bright yellow
	31	2mm	Light apple green

Right Hand Side

10 Climbing Rose

Rajmahal stranded silk - 805, DMC stranded cotton - 502

Silk	33	4mm	Medium blue green
	14	4mm	Deep lemon

11 Red Flowering Foliage

Rajmahal stranded silk - 926, DMC stranded cotton - 502

Silk	74	4mm	Smokey grey green
	50	4mm	Rich deep red

12 Foxgloves

Silk	901	4mm	Very pale sky blue
	125	4mm	Light blue
	44	4mm	Medium sky blue

13 Lily of the Valley

Rajmahal stranded silk - 65, DMC stranded cotton - 319

Silk	21	4mm	Dark forest green
	3	4mm	White

14 Pink Daisies

Silk	20	2mm	Medium grass green
	127	2mm	Light raspberry pink
	15	4mm	Bright yellow

15 Grape Hyacinths

Rajmahal stranded silk - 521, DMC stranded cotton - 470

Silk	171	4mm	Medium olive green
	102	4mm	Deep mauve

16 Lemon Daisies

Silk	21	2mm	Dark forest green
	13	4mm	Pale lemon
	15	4mm	Bright yellow

17 Violets

— as for those listed on Left Hand Side, No. 8

18 Forget Me Knots

Silk	31,	2mm	Light apple green
	125	4mm	Light blue
	15	4mm	Bright yellow

19 Deep Pink Knot Flowers

Rajmahal stranded silk - 926, DMC stranded cotton - 502

Silk	128	4mm	Deep raspberry pink
	74	4mm	Smokey grey green

Background Flower Groupings

Colours used are given in groupings from left to right. Flowers and bushes are created using small ribbon stitches with 2mm ribbon and French knots only.

1 Rajmahal stranded silk - 926, DMC stranded cotton - 3817

Silk	32	2mm	Light blue green
	5	2mm	Pale pink

2 Silk	14	4mm	Deep lemon
	56	2mm	Light mustard green

3 Rajmahal stranded silk - 926, DMC stranded cotton - 3817

Silk	31	2mm	Light apple green
	44	2mm	Medium sky blue
4 Silk	65	2mm	Light caramel
	13	2mm	Pale lemon

Matcham Road

This garden landscape features a rendered brick wall broken by an intricate pair of wrought iron driveway gates. The gates form the central feature of the design and help to create the illusion of distance, drawing the visitor through to the garden beyond.

Rajmahal stranded silk has again been used exclusively in the design but the DMC stranded cotton alternative has been included for your reference should you wish to substitute.

The gates have been worked in Rajmahal stranded silk No. 226, 1 strand.

Applying the Paint

a Using the feature diagram beneath your fabric, mark in the outer edge of the work and the position of the path, using a water erasable pen.

b Using a fine pencil, mark in the details for the gates. These lines are covered with fine stem stitch so keep them as neat as possible.

c Using a brown 'Pygma' pen, lightly mark in the outline of the rendered fence.

d Using the paints 902, 942 and horizontal brush strokes, paint in the path.

e Refer to the flower positioning diagram and gauge where the wash of green 923, 924 needs to be applied to form the background of the flower groups. Much of the fence area is given a green wash of paint as a flower background, as well as the area immediately behind the gates, to create the feeling of depth.

f Refer to the flower positioning diagram to mark in the placement of stems, etc, for each individual flower group.

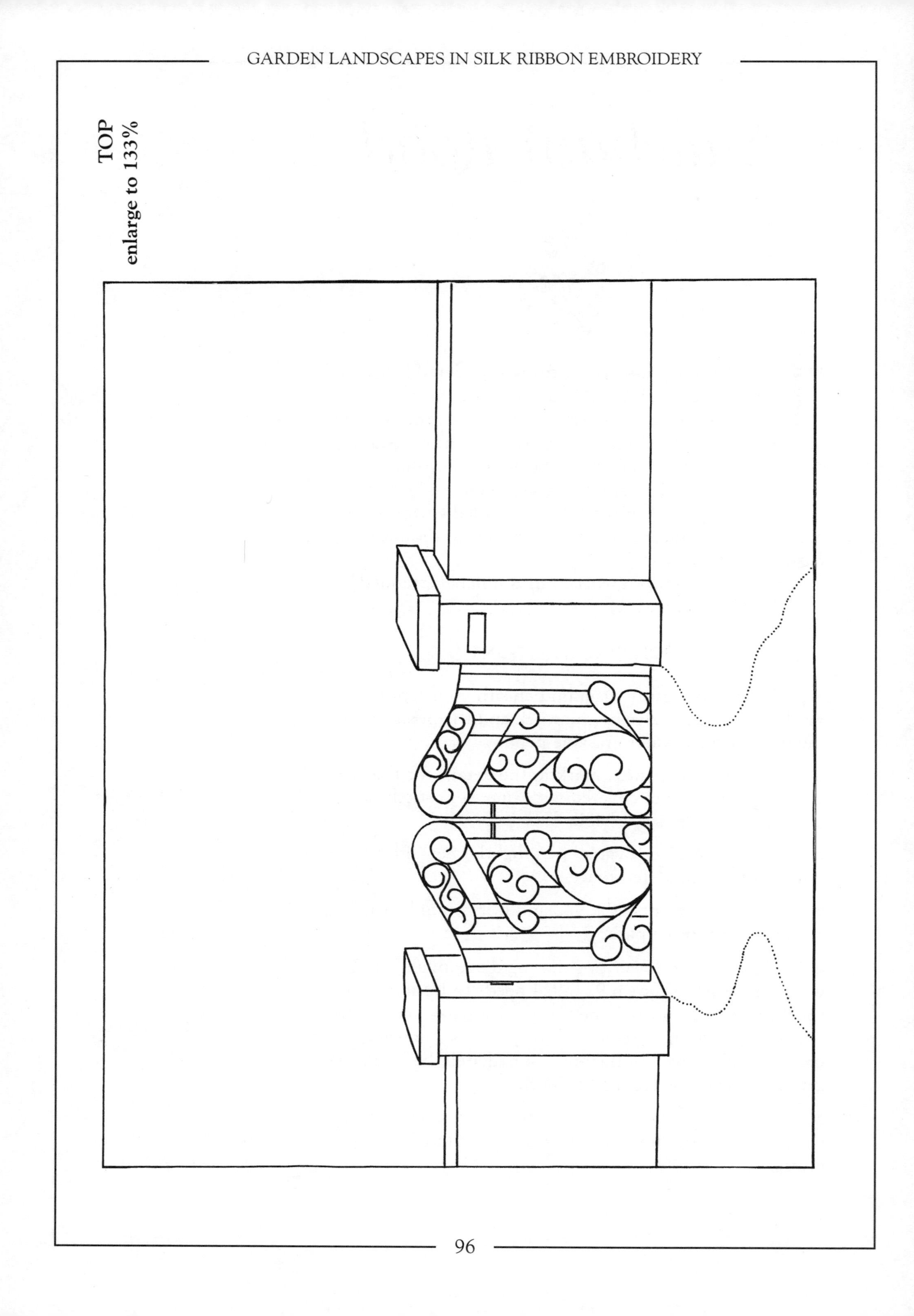
TOP
enlarge to 133%

TOP
enlarge to 133%

g Flowers created in this garden have been listed in two sections: those appearing on the left hand side of the work and those appearing on the right. All threads and ribbons used for each flower grouping are stated on the following pages.

Left Hand Side

1 Magnolia

Rajmahal stranded silk - 521, DMC stranded cotton - 470

Silk	171	4mm	Medium olive green
	50	4mm	Rich deep red
	5	4mm	Very pale pink

2 Pink Flowering Foliage

Rajmahal stranded silk - 926, DMC stranded cotton - 3817

Silk	32	2mm	Light blue green
	8	2mm	Pale pink

3 Daffodils

Rajmahal stranded silk - 805, DMC stranded cotton - 520

Silk	33	2mm	Medium blue green
	15	4mm	Bright yellow
	156	2mm	Dark cream

4 Bluebells

Rajmahal stranded silk - 805, DMC stranded cotton - 319

Silk	21	2mm	Dark forest green
	44	2mm	Medium sky blue

5 Grape Hyacinths

Rajmahal stranded silk - 521, DMC stranded cotton - 734

Silk	170	4mm	Light yellow green
	102	2mm	Deep mauve

6 Dark Pink Daisies

Silk	158	4mm	Medium dusky pink
	13	4mm	Pale lemon
	74	4mm	Smokey grey green

7 Light Pink Daisies

Silk	8	2mm	Pale pink
	128	2mm	Raspberry pink
	31	2mm	Light apple green

Right Hand Side

8 Foliage

Rajmahal stranded silk - 311, DMC stranded cotton - 311

Silk	56	4mm	Light mustard green
Spark Organdy	56	9mm	Used to form additional leaves
	45	9mm	Used to form additional leaves

9 Blue Flowering Foliage

Rajmahal stranded silk - 926, DMC stranded cotton - 3817

Silk	32	4mm	Light blue green
	125	4mm	Light blue

10 Yellow Climbing Rose

Rajmahal stranded silk - 65, DMC stranded cotton - 3346

Silk	21	4mm	Dark forest green
	15	4mm	Bright yellow

11 White Daisy

Rajmahal stranded silk - 521, DMC stranded cotton - 3346

Silk	20	4mm	Medium grass green
	15	4mm	Bright yellow
	1	4mm	Antique white

12 Iris

Rajmahal stranded silk - 926, DMC stranded cotton - 3817
Rajmahal stranded silk - Ecru - to detail straight stitches on flowers

Silk	32	4mm	Light blue green
	179	4mm	Medium grape
	23	4mm	Deep mauve

13 Geranium

Rajmahal stranded silk - 521, DMC stranded cotton - 470

Silk	171	4mm	Medium olive green
	50	4mm	Deep red

14 Dark Pink Daisies

— as for those listed on Left Hand Side, No. 6.

15 Grape Hyacinths

— as for those listed on Left Hand Side, No. 5

16 Violets

Rajmahal stranded silk - 521, DMC stranded cotton - 3346

Silk	20	7mm	Medium grass green
	85	4mm	Deep purple
	15	4mm	Bright yellow

17 Pansies

Rajmahal stranded silk - Ecru, DMC stranded cotton - Ecru

Silk	178	7mm	Medium grape
	21	7mm	Dark forest green
	4	4mm	Black
	15	4mm	Bright yellow

18 Lily of the Valley

Rajmahal stranded silk - 521, DMC stranded cotton - 3346

Silk	20	4mm	Medium grass green
	3	4mm	White

19 Forget Me Knots

Silk	125	4mm	Light blue
	15	4mm	Bright yellow
	31	2mm	Light apple green

20 Deep Red Flowering Foliage

Rajmahal stranded silk - 521, DMC stranded cotton - 3346

Silk	20	2mm	Medium grass green
	130	4mm	Deep burgundy

Stockists

Silk ribbons

Cotton on Creations
Suite 107,
2 Pembroke Street,
Epping, NSW, 2121.
Australia
Phone (02) 8684583, Fax (02) 8684269
(Wholesalers only but if you have difficulty locating the colours required they may be able to help you find a local stockist.)

Timber brooch blanks

Narara Valley Wood turning
Unit 7,
236 Manns Road,
West Gosford, NSW, 2250.
Australia
Phone (043) 232252
(Brooch blanks are available at folk art suppliers, craft shops, etc. or by mail order from the above.)

Stranded silk thread

Rajmahal Art Silks,
Fosterville Road,
Bagshot East, Victoria, 3551.
Australia
Phone (054) 488551, Fax (054) 487044
(Stranded silk is available at many leading craft shops, but if you have difficulty locating a local stockist, Rajmahal Art Silks will be able to give you the details of your local Stockists.)

Don't overlook your local embroidery guild or sewing interest groups for information to help you obtain the supplies you require. Many of their members have years of sewing and embroidery experience and a wealth of knowledge to help source the supplies that you require.

Framing the Garden Landscapes

All of the embroidered landscapes featured here have been professionally framed. It is possible to do this yourself but I feel you will achieve a much more acceptable finish if you entrust your work to a reputable framing gallery. Because of the depth of the embroidered ribbon, tailored spacing has to be inserted between any matt board that you choose to enhance your embroidery and the glass used to keep it free from dust. This spacing prevents the glass from squashing the embroidered flowers.

The embroidered gardens featured have been professionally framed at the Lemon Tree Gallery, East Gosford. My thanks to Pam and Ron for their patience and care.

A final word

As my parting gift to you I have added at the commencement of each chapter a further embroidered brooch design.

They include an illustration which depicts the following flowers:

I have not included colour requirements to produce these designs but I am sure if you have worked your way through my book you will be able to successfully complete each design perhaps as a gift for yourself or a cherished friend. I hope you enjoy embroidering each design.

Helen

Index to Stitches and Flowers

The Stitches

The Flowers